# MEDITERRANEAN DIET COOKBOOK #2020

Easy & Delicious Mediterranean Diet Recipes For Smart People

BY

Francis Michael

COPYRIGHT © 2019 by Francis Michael

ISBN: 978-1-952504-06-8

All rights reserved. This book is copyright protected and it's for personal use only. Without the prior written permission of the publisher, no part of this publication should be reproduced, distributed, or transmitted in any form or by any means, including photocopying, recording, or other electronic or mechanical methods. This publication is sold with the idea that the publisher is not required to render accounting, officially permitted, or otherwise, qualified services. Seek for the services of a legal or professional, a practiced individual in the profession if advice is needed.

## DISCLAIMER

The information contained in this book is geared for educational and entertainment purposes only. Strenuous efforts have been made towards providing accurate, up to date and reliable complete information. The information in this book is true and complete to the best of our knowledge. Neither the publisher nor the author takes any responsibility for any possible consequences of reading or enjoying the recipes in this book. The author and publisher disclaim any liability in connection with the use of information contained in this book. Under no circumstance will any legal responsibility or blame be apportioned against the author or publisher for any reparation, damages, or monetary loss due to the information herein, either directly or indirectly.

# Table of Contents

## INTRODUCTION ............................................................................ 8
Meaning of Mediterranean Diet ................................................. 8
History of the Mediterranean Diet ............................................. 9
The Science Behind the Mediterranean Diet ............................ 10
Health Benefits of Eating the Mediterranean Diet ................... 11
Delicious Path to Weight Loss on Mediterranean diet ............. 13
Foods to Eat On Mediterranean Diet ....................................... 14
Foods to Avoid On Mediterranean Diet ................................... 16
How to Plan your Mediterranean diet ...................................... 17
Tips for Success on Mediterranean Diet .................................. 19
Mediterranean Diet Shopping Guide ....................................... 21
Eating Out on the Mediterranean Diet .................................... 22

## BREAKFAST RECIPES ............................................................. 23
Watermelon Feta & Balsamic Pizzas ........................................ 23
Banana Gingerbread Breakfast Quinoa Bake .......................... 24
Tuna Salad ................................................................................ 25
Greek Omelette Casserole ....................................................... 26
Feta Frozen Yogurt ................................................................... 27
Greek Salad Sushi .................................................................... 28
Egg Muffins with Ham ............................................................. 29
Scrambled Eggs ........................................................................ 30
Zucchini and Tomato Frittata .................................................. 31
Baked Orange French toast with Almond Crumble................ 32
Berry Delicious Fruit Salad ..................................................... 33
Apple and Blueberry Crumble................................................. 34

## LUNCH RECIPES .................................................. 35

Quinoa with Pistachios, Lemon and Mint ........................... 35

Israeli Salad ........................................................ 36

Garlicky Avocado Grilled Cheese with Tomato Pesto ............ 37

Pesto and Garlic Shrimp Bruschetta ............................... 38

Basil Pesto .......................................................... 39

Sweet and Tangy Vinegar Coleslaw ................................ 40

Sweet and Sour Asian Pickled Cucumbers ......................... 41

Chicken Satay with Lighter Almond Dipping Sauce .............. 42

Baked Chicken Meatballs ........................................... 44

Summer Grain Salad ................................................ 45

## DINNER RECIPES ................................................. 46

Warm Caprese Pesto Pasta ......................................... 46

Chipotle Lentil Soup with Avocado ................................ 48

Thai Glazed Salmon with Vegetables .............................. 49

Cheesy Sausage Penne .............................................. 50

Lime Beef and Basil Stir Fry ...................................... 51

Thai Chicken Curry ................................................. 52

15 Minute Lo Mein .................................................. 53

Creamy Tomato Garlic Butter Shrimp ............................. 54

Coq Au Riesling Pasta .............................................. 55

Black Bean Enchilada Pasta ....................................... 56

## SALAD & SOUP RECIPES ........................................ 57

Avocado Caprese Salad ............................................. 57

Asian Ramen Noodle Salad ......................................... 58

Roasted Cauliflower Soup .......................................... 59

Arugula Salad with Shaved Parmesan ............................................... 60

Chicken Salsa Soup ............................................................................ 61

Smokey Chili Mac Soup..................................................................... 62

Avocado, Onion and Tomato Salad.................................................... 63

Thai Chicken Soup.............................................................................. 64

Classic Egg Salad Sandwich ............................................................. 65

Creamy Roasted Tomato Soup........................................................... 66

## POULTRY RECIPES ........................................................................... 67

BBQ Chicken Salad.............................................................................67

Cheesy Chicken and Broccoli Whole Wheat Pasta ................ 69

Chicken Piccata Pasta........................................................................ 70

Buffalo Chicken Grilled Cheese......................................................... 71

Balsamic and Honey Chicken Skewers ...........................................72

Asian Glazed Orange Chicken ..........................................................73

Chicken Nicoise Pasta Salad ............................................................74

Chinese Chicken Salad with Sesame Dressing.........................75

Chicken Caesar Salad ........................................................................76

Chicken Divan Macaroni and Cheese .............................................77

## FISH & SEAFOOD RECIPES ........................................................... 78

Crab Salad Sweet Potato Chip Bites............................................... 78

Citrus Shrimp and Avocado Salad ..................................................79

Baked Salmon with Creme Fraiche................................................. 80

Crab and Shrimp Seafood Cobb Salad ..........................................81

Crab and Avocado Grilled Cheese ................................................. 82

Shrimp Cocktail................................................................................... 83

Blackened Seafood Pasta.................................................................. 84

Chicken, Sausage and Shrimp Jambalaya .............................. 85

Classic Shrimp Macaroni Salad.............................................. 87

Maple Oatmeal with Sweet Potato ......................................... 88

## BEANS, RICE & GRAIN RECIPES ............................ 89

Greek White Bean Soup with Orange Slices ......................... 89

Oatmeal Recipe for Steel Cut Oats ......................................... 90

Beans and Greens over Polenta............................................... 91

Teriyaki Chicken Rice Bowls .................................................. 92

Sweet Corn, Gouda and Farro Risotto ................................... 93

Chicken and Rice Casserole .................................................... 94

Black Eyed Beans and Avocado Salad Crete ......................... 95

Fresh Tomato and Ricotta Whole Wheat Pasta .................... 96

Lemon Rice ................................................................................97

## DESSERT RECIPES ......................................................... 98

Spring Fever and Strawberry Banana Milkshake .................. 98

Raspberry Peach Hand Pies .................................................... 99

Pumpkin Chocolate Chip Cookies ........................................ 100

Dreamy Creamy Mango Pops................................................ 101

Snicker doodles with White Chocolate Chips ......................102

Shortcut Pie Dough Sugar Cookies .......................................103

Raspberries and Cream ..........................................................104

Peach Pie Smoothie ................................................................105

Apple and Oatmeal Rice Krispie Treats ...............................106

Strawberry and Quinoa Parfait .............................................107

## SNACK RECIPES............................................................. 108

Currant Cookies ..................................................................... 108

Pull-Apart Cinnamon Pecan Rolls ........................................109
Apple and Blueberry Crumble................................................ 110
Double Chocolate Zucchini Bread......................................... 111
Chocolate Cream Pie ............................................................. 112
Dark Chocolate Brownies Plus Friday Faves ...................... 113
Cookie S'mores ...................................................................... 114
Stuffed Pizza Rolls ................................................................. 115

# INTRODUCTION

## Meaning of Mediterranean Diet

A Mediterranean diet is a diet of many Mediterranean countries such as Italy and Greece that are mainly of cereals, grains, vegetables, beans, fruits, and nuts with reasonable quantity of fish, cheese, olive oil, and wine. It is usually followed in Greece, Crete, Spain, and parts of Italy that emphasizes fruits and vegetables, nuts, grains, olive oil instead of butter and grilled chicken and seafood with a glass of red wine. Mediterranean diet makes use of fruits, bread, vegetables, cereals, beans, nuts and seeds. Olive oil is used instead of butter and Dairy products, fish and poultry are eaten in moderate quantity. In terms of meat, small quantity is eaten while eggs are at least zero to four times a week.

Scientists stated that a Mediterranean diet plays a good role in the prevention of coronary artery heart disease. It also appears to aid stay away from the metabolic syndrome.

# History of the Mediterranean Diet

The countries that have originated the Mediterranean diet comprise all countries that surround the Mediterranean Sea. In Europe, parts of Italy, Greece, Portugal and Spain stick to ethics of the Mediterranean Diet. Parts of the Balkan region and Turkey follow the diet, as well as Middle Eastern countries like Lebanon and Syria. The warm temperature of the Mediterranean region makes them produce large fresh fruits and vegetables almost year round that people eat across the globe. Bread, olive oil, wine, nuts, and legumes are other food of the region.

However, the diet of the Mediterranean basin about 22countries along the bounds of Africa, Europe, and Asia is rich in foods of plant origin such as legumes, fruits and vegetables, and olive oil as a major basis of fat and consumes minimal saturated fat. There are some few local differences and similarities in terms of patterns of diet around the Mediterranean Sea. Over many decades, Mediterranean diet's origins reflect the relations of various populations and civilizations.

Diet is one of the most important risk factors within our control. This is found about 30% and 20% of the population risk for heart disease and stroke respectively. In modern history, a lot of research has been done concerning the dietary pattern of Mediterranean. Cognitive interest on the Mediterranean diet and lifestyle began in the late 1950s when scientists spotted that Italy, Spain, Southern France, Greece and Turkey experienced fewer deaths from heart disease as found in other countries. They finally resolved that low in takes of saturated fat were the major diet's features that sheltered the hearts of people in the region.

The Mediterranean diet has low saturated fat and is regarded as a low-fat diet. Moderate intake of wine and alcohol and lively lifestyles also define the traditional Mediterranean way of life.

# The Science Behind the Mediterranean Diet

The Mediterranean diet is a current food representation adopted by the usual food patterns of some of the countries of the Mediterranean region, mostly Greece, Cyprus, Portugal, Southern Italy, Turkey and Spain.

Shared features to the diets of these countries are a high consumption of fruit and vegetables, bread and other cereals, olive oil and fish, making those people low in saturated fat and high in dietary fibre.

A major feature in the demand of the Mediterranean Diet is its richness and sweet flavoured foods. Margarine and other butter are considered tasteless and missing the flavour that olive oil gives to meals. Red wine is also taken often but in reasonable quantities. It has been scientifically proven that Mediterranean Diet is one of the low carb diets.

# Health Benefits of Eating the Mediterranean Diet

The following are health benefits of eating the Mediterranean diet; consistently eating the Mediterranean diet exposes us to some benefits that are associated with our health and happy living:

1. **Mediterranean Diet Aids in Preserving Loss of Memory.**

The Mediterranean diet is very good for developing brain power and preventing loss of memory because it is rich in healthy fats for the brain. Researchers and their studies suggest that high devotion to a Mediterranean diet is associated with a 40% reduced risk for loss of memory.

2. **Mediterranean Diet Has Capacity to Manage Diabetes and Blood Sugar Level.**

Researchers have proven that Mediterranean diet has helpful effects for diabetes. In particular, type 2 diabetes can be manage and also help improve blood sugar control. It may not give total cure to diabetes but it can help in managing the sickness.

3. **Mediterranean Diet Aids in Fighting Depression.**

Individuals who adhere to the Mediterranean diet can be protected against depression. Research confirms that a person who follows Mediterranean diet most strictly has lower threat of developing depression.

4. **Mediterranean Diet Guard Against Cancer.**

High consistency to a Mediterranean Diet can help protect against cancer. Research discovers that people who stick to the diet mainly have a 13% rate of cancer death. Particular cancers guarded against include breast cancer, prostate cancer, liver cancer, colorectal cancer, neck cancer and gastric cancer.

5. **Mediterranean Diet Aids in Reducing Your Risk of Having Heart Disease.**

According to research, a Mediterranean diet can significantly cut your risk of having cardiovascular disease, such as myocardial infarction, stroke and coronary heart disease. This is probably as a result of the Mediterranean diet's helpful effects on cardiovascular risk features, such as high blood pressure, triglycerides, and cholesterol. To reduce risk of having Heart disease, Mediterranean diet is a strong recommendation.

6. **Mediterranean Diet Aids in Strengthening Bones.**

According to scientific research, some important elements in olive oil can help in preserving bone density by increasing the large number and give strong bone. Nutritional guide associated with the Mediterranean diet may help to guard against osteoporosis.

7. **Eating Mediterranean Diet May Reduce Women's Risk for Partial Stroke.**

Eating Mediterranean Diet can help to decrease the risk of cardiovascular disease in some women. Well, the diet can also help reduce stroke risk in women. The more closely a woman follows a Mediterranean Diet, the lower the risk of having a stroke.

8. **The Mediterranean Diet May Help In Weight Loss and Maintenance.**

Likely due to its focus on whole grain and fresh foods, the Mediterranean Diet may help you drastically lose weight in a sustainable way.

# Delicious Path to Weight Loss on Mediterranean diet

Here are some tips that will guide you to weight loss on Mediterranean diet.

1. **Eating foods that are main meals should be taken in the early hours of the day.**

Usually in a Mediterranean diet, lunch is the major food. By eating a larger meal early in the day, you reduce the risk of overeating later. According to research people who ate their largest meal before 3 pm are the ones who will lose more weight compared to those that eat largest meal beyond 3pm.

2. **Eat vegetables regularly and as your main food cooked in olive oil.**

When eating a vegetable dish cooked in olive oil and tomato you are taking 4 portions of vegetables in one sitting. Mediterranean dishes are not high in calories but are low in carbs. An added benefit of eating vegetables is that you will avoid drowsiness because it is not a carb rich meal.

3. **Drink mostly water and sometimes tea, coffee and wine for adults.**

In Mediterranean diet you should drink water, rather than milk and yoghurt. To lose weight with Mediterranean diet water must be taken mostly. At times adults could drink tea, coffee and wine while eating, as it aids in weight lose too.

4. **Eat moderate quantity of olive oil.**

Olive oil not only makes all those vegetables delicious, it makes the meal filling. It gives a nice flavour and makes our meal nutritious. It also aids in weight loss.

# Foods to Eat On Mediterranean Diet

Your diet should be according to these healthy and natural Mediterranean foods:

1. **Eggs**:

Chicken, duck eggs and quail.

2. **Dairy**:

Cheese and Greek yogurt

3. **Spices and Herbs**:

Mint, Garlic, basil, rosemary, sage, nutmeg, cinnamon, pepper

4. **Healthy Fats**:

Olives, Extra virgin olive oil, avocados and avocado oil

5. **Drinks:**

Water, Red wine, Coffee, Tea

6. **Vegetables**:

Spinach, onions, cauliflower, Tomatoes, broccoli, kale, carrots, Brussels sprouts, cucumbers

7. **Fruits**:

Apples, bananas, oranges, pears, strawberries, grapes, dates, figs, melons, peaches

8. **Nuts and Seed**s:

Macadamia nuts, hazelnuts, cashews, Almonds, walnuts, sunflower seeds, pumpkin seeds

9. **Legumes**:

Lentils, pulses, Beans, peas, peanuts, and chickpeas

10. **Tubers**:

Potatoes, turnip, yam

11. **Whole grains**:

Barley, corn, buckwheat, Whole oats, brown rice, rye, whole wheat, whole-grain bread and pasta

12. **Fish and Seafood**:

Tuna, mackerel, Salmon, sardines, trout, shrimp, oysters, clams, crab, mussels

13. **Poultry**:

Turkey, chicken, and duck

# Foods to Avoid On Mediterranean Diet

You should avoid these foods while on Mediterranean diet:

1. **Tran's Fats:**

Found in margarine and processed foods.

2. **Refined Oils:**

Canola oil, Soybean oil, cottonseed oil etc

3. **Processed Meat:**

Processed sausages, and hot dogs

4. **Highly Processed Foods:**

Food labelled low- fat and which is factory-made.

5. **Added Sugar:**

Ice cream, Soda, candies, table sugar, and others

6. **Refined Grains:**

Pasta made with refined wheat and White bread etc.

# How to Plan your Mediterranean diet

This is a day to day guide on how to plan your diet to get an effective result.

1. **Monday:**

**Breakfast:** Oats and Greek yogurt with strawberries.

**Lunch:** Vegetables with Whole-grain sandwich

**Dinner:** A piece of fruit and tuna salad, dressed in olive oil

2. **Tuesday:**

**Breakfast:** Raisins with Oatmeal

**Lunch:** Leftover tuna salad from previous night.

**Dinner:** Olives, Salad with tomatoes, and feta cheese.

3. **Wednesday:**

**Breakfast:** Tomatoes, Omelette with veggies, onions and fruit.

**Lunch:** Cheese, Whole-grain sandwich, and fresh vegetables.

**Dinner:** Mediterranean lasagne.

4. **Thursday:**

**Breakfast:** Yogurt, fruits and nuts.

**Lunch:** Leftover lasagne from previous night.

**Dinner:** Brown rice, vegetables and Broiled salmon.

5. **Friday:**

**Breakfast**: Vegetables, and Eggs.

**Lunch**: Oats, Greek yogurt with strawberries, and nuts.

**Dinner**: Grilled lamb, with salad and baked potato.

6. **Saturday:**

**Breakfast**: Nuts, apple, oatmeal with raisins

**Lunch**: vegetables with Whole-grain sandwich.

**Dinner**: Pizza, whole wheat, cheese, vegetables and olives.

7. **Sunday:**

**Breakfast**: Olives, Omelette, and veggies.

**Lunch**: Leftover pizza from the previous night.

**Dinner**: Grilled chicken, with vegetables, potato and fruit.

# Tips for Success on Mediterranean Diet

1. **Change Your Oil:**

Switch vegetable oil and coconut oil to extra-virgin olive oil because olive oil is loaded in monounsaturated fatty acids; according to a 2017 study it may improve HDL cholesterol being the best type of cholesterol. You can sprinkle it on finished foods like fish and chicken. Change butter for olive oil in mashed potatoes, pasta.

2. **Eat Lots of Fish:**

Fish is rich in protein in the Mediterranean diet. Especially, fishes like salmon, sardines and mackerel. These fish are rich in heart and brain healthy fatty acids. Smaller fishes that are thinner and have less fat are also good because they are good source of protein.

3. **Eat Veggies Almost Every day:**

If your diet lacks vegetables, put in more veggies. To do this, eat one serving at snack time, like putting a handful of spinach into a smoothie and one at dinner. Target at least two servings per day. According to Australian research, at least three servings can help you bust stress.

4. **Snack on Nuts:**

This is another Mediterranean diet staple. Nuts include almonds, cashews and pistachios. This can give you some satisfactions. Studies show that if people replaced their snack with almonds, their level of calories, added sugar and sodium will be lower. Nuts have more fibre and minerals for example potassium compared to processed snack foods.

5. **Savour Every Bite:**

Do not rush to eat your meal, calmly sit down at the table with your family and friends and eat properly. It gives you comfort. You will enjoy your company and your food. Eating slowly also gives a lot of satisfaction to your body.

6. **Choose Fruit for Dessert:**

Fruit is a good source of fibre, vitamin C and antioxidants. It helps you to eat more, add a little sugary slice of pear with honey. Always have fruit at your reach in order to satisfy your taste.

7. **Sip a Little Wine:**

The Mediterranean people are known for their consistent drinking of wine to quench their taste. It doesn't mean you should get drunk. It is strongly advised by the Dieticians who developed the Mediterranean diet that women should stick to a 3 Oz. serving, and men to a 5 Oz. serving per day.

8. **Eat Whole Grains:**

Go with grains that are in their whole form and unrefined. Quinoa does not take enough time to cook. It can be cooked in just 20 minutes, making it a great side dish. Use hot oat meal which is best for breakfast on a cold winter morning. Popcorn is also a whole grain. Complement your intake with other whole grain products, like whole wheat bread and pasta.

# Mediterranean Diet Shopping Guide

Below is a simple shopping list to help you begin the Mediterranean Diet.

1. **Vegetables**: Broccoli, spinach, Carrots, onions, kale, garlic
2. **Fruits**: Oranges, grapes, Apples, and bananas
3. **Dairy**: Cheese, Greek yogurt.
4. **Eggs**: Chicken, Pastured enriched eggs.
5. **Oil**: Olive oil.
6. **Berries**: Blueberries and Strawberries
7. **Frozen veggies**: Select combination of healthy vegetables.
8. **Grains**: Whole-grain pasta and Whole-grain bread,
9. **Legumes**: Lentils, pulses, beans.
10. **Nuts**: Cashews, Almonds, walnuts.
11. **Fish**: Shellfish, salmon, sardines, mackerel, trout, shrimp.
12. **Tubers**: Sweet potatoes, yam, and Potatoes
13. **Seeds**: Sunflower seeds, pumpkin seeds.
14. **Condiments**: Cinnamon, sea salt, pepper, turmeric.

# Eating Out on the Mediterranean Diet

The actual food that belongs to the Mediterranean Diet is a great disagreement on global scene. Different countries have their different diet but the focus is on healthy plant foods. Eat the following foods while eating out on Mediterranean Diet with your family and friends:

1. **Oil and Fat**: Extra virgin olive oil, Avocado oil.

2. **Fruits**: Blueberries, grapes, apricots, apples, Bananas, oranges, Peaches, strawberries, raspberries etc.

3. **Whole grains**: pasta, Whole-grain bread, Couscous, barley, corn, Oatmeal etc.

4. **Eggs**: Chicken, and duck eggs.

5. **Dairy**: Plain ricotta, Plain Greek yogurt, feta, goat cheese.

6. **Legumes**: Beans, lentils etc.

7. **Vegetables**: Artichokes, garlic, broccoli, carrots, onions, spinach, Eggplant, bell peppers, zucchini, and etc.

8. **Fish and seafood**: Mackerel, Shrimp, salmon, oysters, Sardines, etc.

9. **Poultry**: Duck, Chicken, turkey etc.

10. **Herbs and spices**: Cinnamon, pepper, garlic, basil, all herbs that are dried and fresh, Spices

11. **Tubers**: Turnips, yams, sweet potatoes, etc.

12. **Nuts and seeds**: Pistachios, cashews, walnuts, almonds etc.

# BREAKFAST RECIPES

## Watermelon Feta & Balsamic Pizzas

Preparation Time: 15 minutes

Total Time: 15 minutes

Serves: 4

**Ingredients**:

- 1 Watermelon sliced
- 1 Oz. crumbled Feta cheese
- 6 Kalamata Olives, sliced
- 1 Tsp. mint leaves
- ½ Tbsp. balsamic glaze

**Cooking Instructions:**

1. Cut the widest part of a round watermelon into two. Place the flat side down on a cutting board and slice. Slice each half into 4 pieces.

2. Put them in a round dish like a pizza and top with cheese, balsamic glaze, mint leaves and olive.

3. Serve and enjoy!!!

## Banana Gingerbread Breakfast Quinoa Bake

Preparation Time: 10 minutes

Cook Time: 1 hour 20 minutes

Total Time: 1 hour 30 minutes

Serves: 8

**Ingredients:**

- 3 Cups of Medium over-ripe one Banana mashed
- ¼ Cup of Molasses
- ¼ Cup of Pure maple syrup
- 1 Tbsp. Cinnamon
- 2 Tsp. Raw vanilla extract
- 1 Tsp. Ground ginger
- 1 Tsp. Ground cloves
- ½ Tsp. Ground allspice
- ½ Tsp. Salt
- 1 Cup of Quinoa uncooked
- 2 ½ Cups of Unsweetened vanilla
- Almond milk
- ¼ Cup of Slivered almonds

**Cooking Instructions:**

1. In the bottom of a casserole dish, mix together the mashed banana, molasses, maple syrup, cinnamon, vanilla extract, ginger, cloves, allspice and salt.

2. Put the quinoa and stir. Put in the almond milk and mix. Cover with the lid and put in a freezer overnight.

3. Preheat your oven to 350ºF in the morning, and mix the quinoa mixture. Cover the pan with tinfoil and bake for about 1 hour 15 mins.

4. Spin your oven to high broil, open the pan, add sliced almonds, and put them into the quinoa and bake for about 4 minutes. Allow to cool for 10 minutes.

5. Serve and enjoy!!!

## Tuna Salad

Preparation Time: 8 minutes

Total Time: 8 minutes

Serves: 2

Calories: 155 kcal

**Ingredients:**

- 1Can Wild Selections solid white albacore tuna water drained
- 2 Tbsp. capers
- 8 kalamata olives sliced
- ¼ Cup of roasted red peppers diced
- 1 Tbsp. lemon juice
- 2 Tbsp. olive oil
- 1 Tbsp. Tablespoon chopped fresh flat-leaf
- Parsley
- Salt and pepper to taste

**Cooking Instructions:**

1. Put all ingredients to a mixing bowl and use a fork to flake apart the tuna and combine together.

2. Serve and enjoy!!!

# Greek Omelette Casserole

Preparation Time: 10 Minutes

Cook Time: 35 Minutes

Total Time: 45 Minutes

**Ingredients:**

- 12 Large eggs
- 2 Cups of whole milk
- 8Oz. fresh spinach
- 2 Cloves garlic, minced
- 12 Oz. artichoke salad with pepper and olive drained and chopped
- 5 Oz. sun dried tomato feta
- Cheese, crumbled
- 1 Tbsp. fresh chopped dill
- 1 Tsp. dried oregano
- 1 Tsp. lemon pepper
- 1 Tsp. salt
- 4 Tsp. olive oil, divided

**Cooking Instructions:**

1. Preheat oven to 375ºF. Cut the fresh herbs and artichoke salad. Put a skillet over medium heat and put 1 Tbsp. olive oil.

2. Sauté spinach and garlic for about 3 minutes. Grease a baking dish and put the spinach and artichoke salad evenly in the dish.

3. Whisk together the eggs, milk, herbs, salt and lemon pepper in a medium bowl.

4. Pour the egg mixture over vegetables and sprinkle with feta cheese. Bake in the oven for 40 minutes.

5. Serve and enjoy!!!

# Feta Frozen Yogurt

Preparation Time: 5minutes

Freezing time: 4 hours

Serves: 1

Calories: 161kcal

**Ingredients:**

- 1 Cup of plain Greek yogurt
- ½ Cup of feta cheese
- 1 Tbsp. Honey

**Cooking Instructions:**

1. Mix together all the available ingredients in a food blender, blend it properly, put into a large plate and refrigerate to be solidified.

2. To blend the frozen mixture, break them into small portion, and place them in the food blender.

3. Put some Tsp. of water. Give it a good blend. Top with honey.

4. Serve and enjoy!!!

# Greek Salad Sushi

Preparation Time: 10 Minutes

Total Time: 10 Minutes

Calories: 54 Kcal.

Serves: 4

## Ingredients:

- Salt and pepper
- ½ Bell pepper, diced
- ¼ Cup of red onion, diced
- ¼ Cup of crumbled feta cheese
- 1 Cucumber
- ½ Cup of plain Greek yogurt
- 2 Tsp. lemon juice
- 1 Clove garlic, minced
- 1 Tsp. fresh dill, chopped

## Cooking Instructions:

1. Trim out the cucumber ends and peel thin slices with a vegetable peeler. Place the slices on a paper towel.

2. Pat dry and keep it aside. Prepare the Tzatziki by mixing together lemon, garlic, yogurt, dill, salt, and pepper.

3. Sprinkle tzatziki on top of the cucumber slice along with onion, pepper and feta. Roll up and lock it with a toothpick. Repeat this for all ingredients.

4. Serve and enjoy!!!

# Egg Muffins with Ham

Preparation Time: 10 minutes

Cook Time 15 minutes

Total Time: 25 minutes

Calories: 109 Kcal.

Serves: 6

## Ingredients:

- 9 Slices of thin cut deli ham
- ½ Cup of Canned roasted red pepper, sliced
- 1/3 Cup of Fresh spinach, minced
- ¼ Cup of Feta cheese, crumbled
- 5 Large eggs
- Pinch of salt
- Pinch of pepper
- 1 ½ Tbsp. Pesto sauce
- Fresh basil for garnish

## Cooking Instructions:

1. Preheat oven to 400°F. Sprinkle cooking spray on a muffin tin. Closely keep 1.5 piece of ham on each of the muffin tin.

2. Put some roasted pepper in the bottom of the muffin tins. Pour 1 Tsp. Spinach on top of the red pepper and finally top with a heaping ½ Tsp. of crumbled feta cheese.

3. Combine together the eggs, salt and pepper. Pour the egg mixture equally into the 6 muffin tins. Bake for 17 minutes.

4. Remove each cup from the muffin tin and top with ¼ Tsp. pesto sauce, and fresh basil.

5. Serve and enjoy!!!

# Scrambled Eggs

Preparation Time: 5 minutes

Cook Time: 10 minutes

Total Time: 15 minutes

Serves: 2

## Ingredients:

- 1 Tbsp. oil
- 1 Yellow pepper, diced
- 2 Spring onions, sliced
- 8 Cherry tomatoes, quartered
- 2 Tbsp. sliced black olives
- 1 Tbsp. capers
- 4 Eggs
- ¼ Tsp. dried oregano
- Black pepper

## Cooking Instructions:

1. Put oil into a frying pan and heat it along with pepper and onions.

2. Sauté for sometimes and put the olives, tomatoes and capers. Sauté for 1 minute.

3. Break the eggs, put in the pan and scramble using a spatula. Put the oregano and plenty of black pepper, and stir continuously.

4. Serve and enjoy!!!

## Zucchini and Tomato Frittata

Preparation Time: 10 minutes

Cook Time 20 minutes

Total Time: 30 minutes

Serves: 4

**Ingredients:**

- 1 Small zucchini, thinly sliced lengthwise
- ½ Cup of yellow or red cherry tomatoes, halved
- 2 Oz. bite-size fresh mozzarella balls
- ⅓ Cup of coarsely chopped walnuts
- 8 Eggs
- ¼ Tsp. salt
- ¼ Tsp. crushed red pepper
- 1 Tbsp. olive oil

**Cooking Instructions:**

1. Preheat your broiler. Combine together the eggs, crushed red pepper and salt in a medium mixing bowl.

2. Using medium high heat, heat olive oil in a skillet. Place zucchini slices on the skillet on equal layer.

3. Cook for about 3 minutes and top with cherry tomatoes. Sprinkle the egg mixture on the vegetables.

4. Put mozzarella balls and walnuts on the top. Cook for about 4 minutes. Slice into wedges.

5. Serve and enjoy!!!

# Baked Orange French toast with Almond Crumble

Preparation Time: 10 minutes

Cook Time: 40 minutes

Total Time: 50 minutes

Serves: 4

## Ingredients:

- 2 Tbsp. sugar
- 1 Tsp. vanilla
- 2 Tbsp. Cointreau
- 1 Tbsp. orange zest
- 1 Loaf challah bread
- 4 Eggs
- 1 Cup of half and half or whole milk

## For Almond Crumble:

- ½ Cup of oats
- 1 Tbsp. orange zest
- ½ Cup of brown sugar
- 4 Tbsp. butter
- ½ Cup of slivered almonds

## Cooking Instructions:

1. Divide the challah bread into ¾ thick slices. Beat the eggs in a 4 Pyrex measuring cup. Put sugar, vanilla, half and half, Cointreau and orange zest.

2. Mix properly. Put butter in the bottom of 2 quart baking pan. Tightly place 6 slices of bread. Sprinkle half of the egg mixture on the bottom layer of bread.

3. Place another layer of bread on the top and sprinkle the remaining mixture. In a small mixing bowl, combine together the butter, almonds, brown sugar, oats and orange zest.

4. Mix properly with your hands. Sprinkle on top of the bread, close with plastic wrap and put in freezer for about 4 hours.

5. Bake for about 40 minutes. Remove from heat and keep for about 5 minutes. Top with raspberry syrup.

6. Serve and enjoy!!!

# Berry Delicious Fruit Salad

Preparation Time: 10 minutes

Total Time: 10 minutes

Serves: 4

## Ingredients:

- 1 Pint blueberries
- 1 Cup of seedless grapes
- ¼ Cup of honey
- Juice of 1 lime
- 1/3 Cup of chopped mint leaves
- 3 Cups of melon such as cantaloupe
- 2 Cups of pineapple cut into chunks
- 3 Oranges 2 of them peeled and sliced into chunks and 1 orange juiced
- 1 Pint raspberries
- 1 Pint strawberries sliced
- 1 Pint blackberries

## Cooking Instructions:

1. In a large mixing bowl, combine the fruit together in a large bowl. Mix the orange juice alongside with the honey and lime juice.

2. Pour on top of the fruit and toss with the mint leaves. Keep it aside for atleast 15 minutes.

3. Serve and enjoy!!!

# Apple and Blueberry Crumble

Preparation Time: 10 minutes

Cook Time: 45 minutes

Total Time: 55 minutes

Serves: 4

## Ingredients:

- ½ Cup of quick oats
- 1 Cup of pecans coarsely chopped
- 6 Tbsp. butter at room temperature
- ¼ Cup of brown sugar
- 4 Gala apples sliced
- 1 Cup of blueberries
- 1 Lemon juiced
- 3 Tbsp. flour
- ½ Cup of sugar
- 1 Tbsp. cinnamon
- 1 Tbsp. butter
- Pinch of kosher salt
- 1 Tsp. cinnamon

## Cooking Instructions:

1. Preheat oven to 350 degrees F. Put butter into a 3-quart baking pan.

2. In a large mixing bowl, put sliced apples along with lemon juice, sugar, flour, cinnamon, blueberries.

3. Mix thoroughly and place the mixture in a baking pan. Mix together the oatmeal, brown sugar, pecans, cinnamon, salt and butter.

4. Mix thoroughly with your hands. Top apple mixture with oatmeal mixture. Bake for about 45 minutes.

5. Serve and enjoy!!!

# LUNCH RECIPES

## Quinoa with Pistachios, Lemon and Mint

Preparation Time: 5 minutes

Cook Time: 15 minutes

Total Time: 20 minutes

Serves: 6

### Ingredients:

- ½ Cup of parsley, chopped
- ¼ Cup of lemon juice
- ¼ Cup of olive oil
- 2 Tsp. salt
- ½ Tsp. pepper
- 2 Tbsp. lemon zest
- 1 Cup of quinoa, rinsed
- ½ Cup of pistachios
- ¼ Cup of currants
- 2 Scallions, finely sliced
- ¼ Cup of Fresh mint leaves, chopped

### Cooking Instructions:

1. Wash quinoa in a fine mesh strainer and mix with 2cups of water and salt in a pan. Cook for about 15minutes.

2. Spread it out on a baking sheet to cool once quinoa is done. Mix quinoa with pistachios, herbs, currants, lemon zest, scallions, juice and olive oil in a big bowl.

3. Put in salt and pepper.

4. Serve and enjoy!!!

# Israeli Salad

Prep Time: 10 minutes

Cook Time: 5 minutes

Total Time: 15 minutes

Serves: 6

## Ingredients:

- 1 Tsp. honey
- 1/3 Cup of lemon juice
- 2 Tbsp. red wine vinegar
- 1 Tsp. sumac
- 2 Tsp. salt
- 1 Tsp. pepper
- 3 Tomatoes
- 4 Cucumbers
- 1 Bell pepper
- 2 Scallions
- 2 Tbsp. parsley, minced
- 1/3 Cup of Olive oil

## Cooking Instructions:

1. Remove seed and finely cut bell pepper, tomatoes, and cucumbers.
2. Cut scallions thinly. In a medium bowl, put vegetables and herbs.
3. Mix together olive oil, honey, lemon juice, sumac, salt, vinegar and pepper.
4. Put into the vegetable mixture and throw to mix.
5. Serve and enjoy!!!

# Garlicky Avocado Grilled Cheese with Tomato Pesto

Preparation Time: 10 minutes

Cook Time: 7 minutes

Total Time:

Serves: 4

**Ingredients:**

- 2 Slices whole wheat white bread
- 1 Tbsp. sun dried tomato pesto
- ½ Avocado mashed
- 5 slices provolone cheese
- 1 Tsp. olive oil
- 3 Tbsp. salted butter
- 2 Tsp. onion powder
- 1 Tsp. garlic powder
- 1 Tsp. kosher salt
- 1 Tsp. dried thyme

**Cooking Instructions:**

1. Mix the butter, garlic powder, kosher salt, onion powder, dried thyme and mash together in a bowl.

2. Put butter mixture on one side of each slice of bread, and then turn over the bread buttered side down.

3. Lay the bottoms slice of bread with a few slices of provolone, and then put the mashed avocado and the sun dried tomato pesto.

4. Add the remaining provolone cheese and the other piece of bread. Spread with the butter mixture. Put a large non-stick pan over low heat.

5. Put the olive oil and a little extra butter mixture. Put the sandwich and cover. Cook for about 4 minutes. Turn over the sandwich and cook for 3 minutes.

6. Serve and enjoy!!!

# Pesto and Garlic Shrimp Bruschetta

Preparation Time: 5 minutes

Cook Time: 5 minutes

Total Time: 10 minutes

Serves: 16

**Ingredients:**

- 1 Oz. feta cheese crumbled
- 20 small fresh basil leaves,
- Delallo Glaze Balsamic
- 8 Oz. 51/60 raw shrimp shell-on, fresh
- Kosher salt and freshly ground black pepper
- 4 Tbsp. extra virgin olive oil divided
- 2 Tbsp. butter
- 4 Cloves garlic minced
- 1 French bread
- 3 Oz. DeLallo Simply Pesto
- 3 Oz. DeLallo sun-dried tomatoes in oil slivered
- 2 Oz. DeLallo capers, drained

**Cooking Instructions:**

1. Take the shells and tails from the shrimp and put in a bowl. Spices with kosher salt and freshly ground black pepper.

2. Put 2 Tbsp. olive oil and 2 Tbsp. butter and cook in a sauté pan over medium heat. Put the garlic and cook for 1 minute.

3. Put the shrimp and cook slowly, turn once, about 4 minutes. Put off the heat and allow the shrimp sit in the garlic oil.

4. Slice the bread. Put on a baking sheet and brush with the remaining olive oil and toast in the oven.

5. Spread each slice of bread with 1 Tsp. of pesto sauce and with sun-dried tomatoes, 2 garlic, and shrimp with sauce, capers, feta cheese and basil leaves. Sprinkle with balsamic glaze.

6. Serve and enjoy!!!

## Basil Pesto

Preparation Time: 5 minutes

Total Time: 5 minutes

Serves: 16

Calories: 102 kcal

**Ingredients:**

- ½ Cup of toasted pine nuts
- ½ Cup of fresh grated Parmesan
- Cheese plus more for garnish
- 1 Garlic clove roughly chopped
- 2 Cups of fresh basil leaves washed, stemmed and finely packed
- ½ Cup of olive oil
- ½ Lemon juiced
- ½ Tsp. kosher salt
- ½ Tsp. freshly ground black pepper

**Cooking Instructions:**

1. Put the chopped garlic, toasted pine nuts and parmesan cheese in the bowl for a food processor and process.

2. Put the basil. Pulse a few times then let it run as you sprinkle the olive oil into the processor as it runs.

3. Spices with kosher salt and freshly ground black pepper, add a squeeze of lemon juice, and mix. Taste and adjust spices.

4. Serve and enjoy!!!

# Sweet and Tangy Vinegar Coleslaw

Preparation Time: 20 minutes

Freezing Time: 1 hour

Total Time: 1 hour 20 minutes

Serves: 12

Calories: 86 kcal

**Ingredients:**

- 10 Cups shredded coleslaw mix
- 1 Cup thinly sliced red onion
- 1 Cup shredded red cabbage
- 1 Carrot thinly slivered
- 1/3 Cup canola oil
- ¼ Cup apple cider vinegar
- 1 Tbsp. sugar
- 1 Tsp. caraway seeds
- 1 Tsp. celery seed
- 1 Tsp. kosher salt
- ½ Tsp. freshly ground black pepper

**Cooking Instructions:**

1. Mix the coleslaw with the red onion, shredded red cabbage, and carrot in a large bowl.

2. Mix the canola oil, apple cider vinegar, caraway seeds, celery seed, kosher salt, sugar and freshly ground black pepper in a small bowl.

3. Pour canola mixture over the cabbage mixture and throw. Cover with a lid and refrigerate for 1 hour.

4. Serve and enjoy!!!

# Sweet and Sour Asian Pickled Cucumbers

Preparation Time: 5 minutes

Freezing Time: 30 minutes

Total Time: 35 minutes

Serves: 10

Calories: 74 kcal

**Ingredients:**

- 1 Tsp. Kosher salt
- 1/8 Tsp. Dried red chile flakes
- 2 Seedless English cucumbers
- 1 Shallot
- 1 Cup seasoned rice vinegar
- ¾ Cup sugar
- 1 Tbsp. Grated ginger

**Cooking Instructions:**

1. Cut the cucumbers into very thin coins and slice the shallot into thin slices. Put both to a medium size bowl.

2. Whisk the rice vinegar, sugar, grated ginger, salt and chile flakes together In a smaller bowl and pour over the cucumbers, toss to coat.

3. Cover with a lid and refrigerate for at least 30 minutes.

4. Serve and enjoy!!!

# Chicken Satay with Lighter Almond Dipping Sauce

Preparation Time: 30 minutes

Cook Time: 37 minutes

Total Time: 1 hour 7 minutes

Serves: 10

**Ingredients:**

**For The Chicken Satay:**

- 2 Boneless skinless chicken breasts
- Canola oil
- Fresh minced cilantro
- Wooden skewers
- 2 Tbsp. good quality fish sauce
- 1 Tbsp. low sodium soy sauce
- 3 Tbsp. minced lemongrass
- 3 Cloves pressed

**For the Almond Dipping Sauce:**

- 3 Tbsp. minced or grated fresh ginger
- 3 Tbsp. brown sugar
- 2 Tbsp. soy sauce
- 1Tsp. crushed red chile flakes to taste
- 1 Cup of Almond Breeze Almond milk
- Coconut milk Original
- ¾ Cup of smooth almond butter
- ¼ Cup of fish sauce

**Cooking Instructions:**

1. Put fish sauce, soy sauce, lemongrass, garlic and combine in a large bowl. Cut the chicken breasts into thin pieces.

2. Put them in the bowl with the marinade. Wrap with plastic cover and refrigerate for at least 30 minutes.

3. Set up a clean grill for high heat and brush the grates with a few paper towels soak with canola oil.

4. Soak wooden skewers in water for 30 minutes. Thread the chicken slices onto the skewers and throw away any of the remaining marinades.

5. To make the dipping sauce. Put all of the ingredients to the bowl of a food processor and process, and then transfer to serving bowls.

6. Put the chicken skewers on the hot grill and cook untouched on high heat for 4 minutes each side.

7. Flip the chicken and cook for another 3minutes, flip a few more times. Drizzle with cilantro and serve with the almond dipping sauce.

8. Serve and enjoy!!!

# Baked Chicken Meatballs

Preparation Time: 10 minutes

Cook Time: 24 minutes

Total Time: 34 minutes

Serves: 6

**Ingredients:**

- ½ Tsp. granulated garlic
- ½ Tsp. granulated onion
- 1 Tsp. salt
- 1 Tsp. pepper
- 1 ½ Lbs. Ground chicken
- ¼ Cup of feta, crumbled
- 1 ½ Tsp. dill, dried
- ¼ Cup of breadcrumbs

**Cooking Instructions:**

1. Preheat oven to 350°F. Combine all ingredients gently in a medium bowl.
2. Using a scoop measure out 2Tbsp. of meatball mixture and roll into a ball.
3. Put meatballs on parchment lined sheet pan and bake at 350°F for 24 minutes.
4. Cool for 5 minutes.
5. Serve and enjoy!!!

# Summer Grain Salad

Preparation Time: 10 minutes

Total Time: 10 minutes

Serves: 10

## Ingredients:

- 1 Cup of barley, cooked
- 1 Cup of freekeh, cooked
- 1 Cup of brown rice, cooked
- 1 ½ Cups of English cucumber, diced
- 2 Cups of grape tomatoes, halved
- 1 Cup of bell peppers, diced
- 1 Cup of rainbow carrots, shredded
- ¼ Cup of fresh dill, finely chopped
- 1/8 Cup of fresh chives, finely chopped
- ½ Cup of flat-leaf parsley, chopped
- 1 ½ Tsp. Kosher salt
- ½ Tsp. Ground black pepper
- 1/3 Cup of red wine vinegar
- 1/4 Cup of olive oil
- Zest and juice of 1 lemon

## Cooking Instructions:

1. Cook grains and set aside to cool completely.

2. Combine vinegar, oil, salt and pepper together in a small bowl, mix and set aside.

3. Combine grains with vinaigrette in a large bowl and mix. Fold in vegetables and herbs.

4. Serve and enjoy!!!

# DINNER RECIPES

## Warm Caprese Pesto Pasta

Preparation Time: 10 minutes

Cook Time: 10 minutes

Total Time: 20 Minutes

Serves: 6

**Ingredient:**

**Caprese Pasta:**

- 2 Boxes Chicka pea Pasta shells
- 2 Tsp. olive oil
- 2 Pints cherry tomatoes
- 1 Mozzarella ball, torn into pieces
- Grated parmesan cheese

**Lemony Pesto:**

- 1 Cup of basil leaves, packed
- ½ Cup of toasted nuts
- ½ Cup of grated parmesan cheese
- ½ Cup of olive oil
- ½ Cup of water
- ¼ Cup of parsley
- 2 Garlic cloves
- Juice of 2 lemon

**Cooking Instructions:**

1. Boil a large pot of salted water. Put the Chicka pea Pasta shells and stir as you put them into the pot.

2. Cook the pasta for 9 minutes then drain and keep aside. While boiling the water, prepare the pesto.

3. Put all the pesto ingredients into your blender and blend on high. Put the oil in a large sauté pan over medium-high heat.

4. Put the cherry tomatoes and quickly throw to dredge them in the oil. Allow them cook for 2 minutes.

5. Shake the pan and cook them for another 2 minutes. Take the pan from the heat.

6. Put the cooked pasta, the mozzarella, and the pesto to the pan and combine. Top with a little freshly grated parmesan cheese.

7. Serve and enjoy!!!

# Chipotle Lentil Soup with Avocado

Preparation Time: 20minutes

Cook time: 10hours

Total time: 10hours 20minutes

Serves: 6

**Ingredients:**

- ½ Yellow onion, chopped
- 2 Celery stalks diced
- 2 Carrots chopped
- 3 Garlic cloves minced
- 2 Cups of brown lentils
- 1½ Tsp. ground cumin
- 1 Tsp. ground oregano
- 1 Chipotle pepper seeded & minced
- 7 Cups of vegetable broth
- 114 Oz. can petite diced tomatoes
- 1 Tsp. adobo sauce from chipotle can
- 1 California avocado chopped
- 2 Tsp. lime juice
- ¼ Cup of minced flat-leaf parsley

**Cooking Instructions:**

1. Mix the onion, celery, lentils, cumin, oregano, carrots, garlic, and chipotle peppers in a slow cooker.

2. Put the vegetable broth, diced tomatoes and adobo sauce. Cook on low for about 10 hours.

3. Flip 3 cups of the soup to a blender and allow cool for about 15 minutes. Put the avocado in the blender and blend.

4. Put the mixture back into the slow cooker. Mix in the lime juice and parsley.

5. Serve and enjoy!!!

## Thai Glazed Salmon with Vegetables

Preparation Time: 5 minutes

Cook Time: 25 minutes

Total Time: 30 minutes

### Ingredients:

- 4 Salmon fillets
- 1 Red bell pepper, chopped
- 1 Green bell pepper, chopped
- 1 Yellow pepper, chipped
- 1 Onion, chopped
- 1 Cup snow peas
- Carrots, thinly sliced
- ½ Cup Thai sweet chili sauce
- ¼ Cup soy sauce
- 1 Tbsp. fresh grated ginger
- 1 Tbsp. fresh lime juice
- Pinch of red pepper flakes
- Chopped cilantro and lime slices for garnish

### Cooking Instructions:

1. Preheat oven to 375ºF and spray a cooking sheet with cooking spray. Place the salmon skin side down surrounded by sliced vegetables.

2. Mix together Thai sweet chili sauce, lime juice, soy sauce, ginger and red pepper flakes in a small bowl.

3. Remain ¼ cup of the marinade and sprinkle the rest of the marinade over the salmon and vegetables. Cover with foil and bake for 15minutes.

4. Remove foil and broil for another 7 minutes. Remove salmon from the oven and brush remaining marinade on top.

5. Garnish with fresh cilantro and lime slices.

6. Serve and enjoy!!!

## Cheesy Sausage Penne

Preparation Time: 10 minutes

Cook Time: 20 minutes

Total Time: 30 minutes

Servings: 4

Calories: 1025 kcal

**Ingredients:**

- 1.5 Cups of chicken or vegetable stock
- ½ Tsp. salt
- ¼ Tsp. black pepper
- 1 Cup of shredded cheddar cheese
- 1 Cup of shredded Pepper Jack cheese
- Chopped basil for garnish
- 2 Tbsp. olive oil
- 1 Medium yellow onion chopped
- 2 Garlic cloves minced
- 1 Medium carrot grated
- 1 Lbs. mild Italian sausage casings removed
- 3 Cups of uncooked penne pasta
- 2 Cups of crushed tomatoes

**Cooking Instructions:**

1. Preheat oil in large skillet. Put chopped onion and minced garlic and sauté on medium heat for 2 minutes.

2. Put shredded carrot and sauté. Put sausage and cook, breaking it up with a wooden spatula. Add pasta, crushed tomatoes and stock to pot.

3. Give everything a good stir. Spice with salt and pepper and boil. Lower the heat to simmer. Cover and cook, stir often.

4. Take from heat and open pot. Top with shredded cheese. Cover for 3minutes.

5. Serve and enjoy!!!

# Lime Beef and Basil Stir Fry

Preparation Time: 15 minutes

Cook Time: 15 minutes

Total Time: 30 minutes

Serves: 4

Calories: 420 kcal

**Ingredients:**

**Stir fry:**

- 12 Oz. steaks 400g total, cut into small pieces
- 1 Cup of basil leaves
- 2 Tbsp. olive oil
- 3 Cloves garlic minced
- 1 Tsp. minced ginger
- 6 Cups of vegetables broccoli, snap peas, and bell pepper

**Sauce:**

- 3 Tbsp. brown sugar
- Juice of 2 limes 3 tablespoons
- 1 Tsp. Corn starch rice to serve
- 2 Tbsp. soy sauce
- 1 Tbsp. fish sauce

**Cooking Instructions:**

1. Preheat oil in a large pan over medium heat. Put garlic and ginger and cook for 1 minute. Put vegetables and cook for 8 minutes.

2. Take the vegetables from the pan and keep aside. Put the steak in the pan, and cook for 3 minutes. Remove steak from pan.

3. Remove any extra oil from the pan. Put the sauce in the pan and cook for 1 minute. Return the steak and vegetables to the pan, with the basil leaves.

4. Throw to dredge. Top over rice.

5. Serve and enjoy!!!

# Thai Chicken Curry

Preparation Time: 10 minutes

Cook Time: 4 hours

Total Time: 4 hours 10 minutes

Serves: 4

**Ingredients:**

- 3 Garlic cloves, minced
- 1 Lbs. boneless, skinless chicken thighs
- 1 Large kabocha, cut into 1-inch cubes
- 1 Medium yellow onion, chopped
- 2 Chili peppers,
- 1 Large bunch of kale, torn into small pieces
- cilantro, chili peppers, and lime to serve
- 1 14 Oz. can coconut milk
- 1 ¾ Cup of water
- 4 Tbsp. Thai red curry paste
- 1 Tbsp. soy sauce
- 1 Tbsp. palm or coconut sugar
- 1 Tbsp. minced ginger
- 2 Tsp. fish sauce

**Cooking Instructions:**

1. Put all the ingredients, except for the kale, into your crock pot and mix. Set your crock pot to cook on high heat for 4hours.

2. After 4 hours, put the kale and keep while you prepare the rice, cauliflower rice to serve. Top with a little cilantro, lime, and some chopped chili peppers.

3. Serve and enjoy!!!

## 15 Minute Lo Mein

Preparation Time: 10 minutes

Cook Time: 5 minutes

Total Time: 15 minutes

**Sauce:**

- 1 Tsp. sesame oil
- 1 Tsp. sugar
- 2 Tbsp. pearl river bridge dark soy sauce
- 1 Tbsp. Pearl River Bridge light soy sauce

**Lo Mien:**

- 6 Oz. uncooked ramen noodles
- 1 Tbsp. sesame oil
- 3 Green onions, chopped
- 3 Cups of julienne vegetables like carrots, red peppers, cabbage, bok choy, mushrooms, or broccoli
- 2 Tbsp. mirin

**Cooking Instructions:**

1. For the sauce, mix all the sauce ingredients together in a jar. Properly cook the noodles and drain and keep aside.

2. Preheat the sesame oil in a large skillet. Put the green onions and vegetables in the hot pan. Stir fry for about5 minutes.

3. Put the mirin to loosen the browned bits up from the bottom of the pan. Put the cooked noodles and half of the sauce, toss to mix.

4. Top with remaining green onions.

5. Serve and enjoy!!!

# Creamy Tomato Garlic Butter Shrimp

Preparation Time: 10 minutes

Cook Time: 5 minutes

Total Time: 15 minutes

Serve: 4

**Ingredients:**

- 400 g bottle passata
- Half a chicken bouillon cube , crushed
- 2 Tbsp. fresh chopped parsley
- 1 Tsp. freshly-ground black pepper, divided
- Pinch of granulated sugar
- 2/3 Cup of milk
- Grated Parmesan cheese
- Extra fresh chopped parsley
- 10 Oz. dry weight linguini
- 1 Medium yellow onion diced
- 2 Tbsp. butter
- 6 Garlic cloves , minced
- 1 Lbs. raw jumbo shrimp, peeled and deveined
- 2 Tsp. dried basil
- 1 Tsp. salt , divided

**Cooking instructions:**

1. Cook pasta al dente and properly drain and keep aside. Preheat the butter in a large pan over medium heat. Put onion and fry.

2. Put garlic and fry for about 30 seconds, then put the shrimp with the basil and ½ Tsp. salt. Sauté shrimp for 2 minutes on one side.

3. Turn and sauté on the other side for more minute. Put the sauce, pepper, sugar, crushed bullion, parsley, and remaining salt.

4. Allow the sauce to heat for another minute before putting the milk. Continue cooking for more minute.

5. Once the pasta is cooked and drained, mix it with the creamy tomato sauce, and toss.

6. Serve and enjoy!!!

# Coq Au Riesling Pasta

Preparation Time: 10 minutes

Cook Time: 20 minutes

Total Time: 30 minutes

Serves: 6

**Ingredients:**

- 3 Garlic cloves sliced
- 1 Cup of dry white wine
- 1 Cup of cream small handful fresh parsley finely chopped
- 2 Tbsp. lemon juice To taste
- Salt & pepper to taste
- 1 Lbs. cooked penne pasta
- 4 Skinless de-boned chicken breasts
- 1 Tbsp. butter
- 2 Tbsp. olive oil
- 2 Cups of portabellini/chestnut mushrooms, sliced

**Cooking Instructions:**

1. Lay the chicken breasts on a cutting board. With a sharp knife, slice the chicken into two thin chicken cutlets.

2. Preheat a large frying pan and melt together the butter and olive oil. Put the chicken breasts in the pan.

3. Cook for two minutes on both sides, spice with salt and pepper. Remove from the pan and set aside. Put a little more oil if necessary.

4. Put the mushrooms in the pan. Allow to brown before adding the garlic and cook for another minute.

5. Put in the wine then keep aside for 2 minutes before putting in the cream. Spice with salt and pepper, put the parsley and lemon juice and cook for 5 minutes.

6. Cut the chicken into strips then add to the sauce with the penne. Put in a little of the pasta cooking water and mix everything in the sauce. Adjust spices.

7. Serve and enjoy!!!

# Black Bean Enchilada Pasta

Preparation Time: 10 minutes

Cook Time: 15 minutes

Total Time: 25 minutes

Serves: 4

**Ingredients:**

- 1 Cup of sweet corn
- 1 Can diced tomatoes
- 1 Cup of enchilada sauce
- 2 Tbsp. taco seasoning
- 4 Cups of water or broth
- ½ Cup of shredded cheddar
- Cilantro, cherry tomatoes, lime wedges
- 4 Cups of small pasta shapes
- 1 Can black beans
- 1 Yellow pepper diced
- 1 Red pepper diced

**Cooking Instructions:**

1. Put all ingredients except for the cheese and garnishes in a big pot. Cover and boil. Open and simmer for about 15 minutes.

2. Put cheese and add more on top. Top with cilantro, diced tomatoes and lime wedges.

3. Serve and enjoy!!!

# SALAD & SOUP RECIPES

## Avocado Caprese Salad

Preparation Time: 10 minutes

Total Time: 10 minutes

Serves: 4

- 1 Tbsp. extra virgin olive oil
- 1 ½ Tsp. balsamic vinegar
- Pinch of sugar
- Kosher salt and freshly ground black pepper
- 2 Cups of fresh arugula
- 3 Campari or cocktail style
- Tomatoes sliced
- ½ Avocado pitted and sliced
- 3 Slices fresh mozzarella cheese
- Fresh basil leaves

**Cooking Instructions:**

1. Combine the arugula, tomato, avocado slices and mozzarella in a bowl. Top with torn basil leaves.

2. Mix the extra virgin olive oil in a bowl with the balsamic vinegar, sugar and spice with kosher salt and freshly ground black pepper to taste.

3. Top over the salad. Throw to coat.

4. Serve and enjoy!!!

# Asian Ramen Noodle Salad

Preparation Time: 10 minutes

Total Time: 10 minutes

Serves: 4

**Ingredients:**

- 1 16- Oz. package coleslaw mix
- 1 Package dry ramen noodles
- 1 15- Oz. can mandarin oranges drained
- 1 Cup frozen shelled edamame beans, thawed
- 6 Green onions whites and greens, chopped
- ¼ Cup slivered almonds
- 1 Tbsp. black sesame seeds
- 7 Tbsp. seasoned rice vinegar
- 2 Tbsp. vegetable oil
- 3 Tsp. light soy sauce
- 3 Tsp. sugar
- 4 Tsp. sesame oil
- Freshly ground black pepper

**Cooking Instructions:**

1. Put the coleslaw mix in a big bowl. Crush the dry ramen noodles into the coleslaw and then put mandarin oranges and edamame.

2. Put the green onions, slivered almonds and black sesame seeds and mix. Mix the rice, vinegar, vegetable oil, soy sauce, sugar, and sesame oil.

3. Add the freshly ground black pepper in a bowl. Sprinkle over the slaw mix and combine. Refrigerate for 1 hour.

4. Serve and enjoy!!!

# Roasted Cauliflower Soup

Preparation Time: 10 minutes

Cook Time: 1 hour

Total Time: 1 hour 10 minutes

Serves: 4

**Ingredients:**

- 1 Cup of chicken stock
- 1 Lemon
- Minced parsley, for garnish
- Fresh parmesan, for garnish
- Coarse salt and pepper
- 2 Heads cauliflower, broken into florets
- 6 Cloves garlic
- 2 Tbsp. extra-virgin olive oil
- 1½ Cup of milk

**Cooking Instructions:**

1. Preheat your oven to 400ºF. Prepare the cauliflower florets on a big baking sheet. Put the garlic cloves on the sheet with the florets.

2. Sprinkle with the olive oil, and a pinch of salt. Toss, and roast for an hour, tossing at the 45-minute mark.

3. Remain about ½ a cup of roasted florets to the side, and flip the rest to a blender. Press the garlic out of its skins right into the blender.

4. Put the milk, stock, and juice from half the lemon. Spice with a pinch of salt and pepper; blend. Flip the soup to a pot and simmer on medium.

5. Measure the soup among small bowls, and garnish with reserved florets, a drizzle of parsley and parmesan cheese.

6. Put a grind of black pepper and a squeeze of lemon juice. Top on a roast chicken and a steamed green.

7. Serve and enjoy!!!

# Arugula Salad with Shaved Parmesan

Preparation Time: 5 minutes

Total Time: 5 minutes

Serves: 2

**Ingredients:**

- ¼ Cup of shaved Parmesan cheese
- 2 Tbsp. olive oil
- 2 Tbsp. fresh lemon juice
- 1 Tsp. honey
- ½ Tsp. kosher salt
- ½ Tsp. freshly ground black pepper
- 4 Cups of arugula

**Cooking Instructions:**

1. Mix together the olive oil, lemon juice, honey, and salt and pepper in a large bowl.

2. Put the arugula in the bowl and toss. Top with the shaved Parmesan and pepper taste.

3. Serve and enjoy!!!

# Chicken Salsa Soup

Preparation Time: 10 minutes

Cook Time: 24 minutes

Total Time: 34 minutes

Serves: 6

**Ingredients**

- 1 Cup of salsa
- 1 Cup of guacamole salsa
- 2 Cups of frozen corn
- 4 Cups of chicken stock
- Coarse salt
- Cilantro, for garnish
- 22 Oz. chicken thighs
- 2 Tbsp. cumin
- 1 Tbsp. chili powder
- 4 Tbsp. extra-virgin olive oil, divided
- 1 Can navy beans, drained and rinsed
- 4 Oz. softened cream cheese

**Cooking Instructions:**

1. Heat oil in a big pot over medium-high heat. Spice the chicken on both sides with salt, cumin and chilli powder.

2. Cook in the pot for about four minutes each side. Remove the chicken from the pot. Preheat your oven. Lay the frozen corn on a baking sheet.

3. Sprinkle 2 Tbsp. oil over it, add a pinch of salt. Coat the corn with oil. Cook for 10 minutes. Put the salsas, the stock and the softened cream cheese in the pot.

4. Mix the soup. Put the beans, chicken and corn to the soup and allow simmering about 10 minutes.

5. Using a fork, slice the chicken, then put it back in the soup. Scoop up, garnish with cilantro.

6. Serve and enjoy!!!

# Smokey Chili Mac Soup

Preparation Time: 10 minutes

Cook Time: 10 minutes

Total Time: 20 minutes

Serves: 6

**Ingredients**:

- 1 Can fire-roasted tomatoes
- 6 Cups of chicken stock
- 1 ¼ Cup of elbow macaroni
- 5 Cups of chopped kale
- 2 Tsp. smoked paprika
- 1 Can pinto beans, drained and rinsed
- 1 Heaping Tbs. tomato paste
- 2 Cups of shredded cheddar cheese
- Parsley, for garnish
- Coarse salt
- 1 Lbs. grass-fed beef
- ½ Large white onion, chopped
- 4 Cloves garlic, minced

**Cooking Instructions:**

1. Brown the beef using a wooden spoon in a large pot. Put the chopped onion, garlic and a pinch of salt. Cook for 3 minutes.

2. Put the smoked paprika and turn. Put the pinto beans and mix. Put the mix to the side and put the tomato paste.

3. Mash the paste into the pot with a wooden spoon, allowing it break up, just about a minute. Then mix the paste into the meat and beans.

4. Put the fire-roasted tomatoes and stock. Bring it to simmer, and put the pasta. Once the pasta reaches al dente, six minutes, put the kale.

5. Scoop the soup into bowls and top with shredded cheddar cheese, and a little parsley.

6. Serve and enjoy!!!

# Avocado, Onion and Tomato Salad

Preparation Time: 10 minutes

Total Time: 10 minutes

Serves: 4

**Ingredients:**

- 6 Cherry tomatoes halved
- Sprig of fresh tarragon
- 1 T fruity olive oil
- ½ Tsp. champagne vinegar
- 1 Large tomato sliced in thick slices
- ½ Avocado sliced
- 2 Slices red onion

**Cooking Instructions:**

1. Add tomatoes, avocado and sliced onion to a small plate, drizzle with tarragon leaves and sprinkle with the olive oil and vinegar.

2. Put kosher salt and some pepper to taste. Put more olive oil.

3. Serve and enjoy!!!

# Thai Chicken Soup

Preparation Time: 10 minutes

Cook Time: 4 hour 30 minutes

Total Time: 4 hour 40 minutes

Serves: 6

**Ingredients:**

- 2 Tbsp. red curry paste
- 2 12 Oz. cans of coconut milk
- 2 Cups of chicken stock
- 2 Tbsp. fish sauce
- 2 Tbsp. brown sugar
- 2 Tbsp. peanut butter
- 1 ½ Lbs. chicken breasts cut into 1 ½ inch pieces
- 1 Red bell pepper seeded and sliced into ¼ inch slices
- 1 Onion thinly sliced
- 1 Heaping tablespoon fresh ginger minced
- 1 Cup of frozen peas thawed
- 1 Tbsp. lime juice
- Cilantro for garnish
- Cooked white rice

**Cooking Instructions:**

1. Combine the curry paste, coconut milk, chicken stock, fish sauce, brown sugar and peanut butter in a slow cooker bowl.

2. Put the chicken breast, onions, red bell pepper, and ginger in the slow cooker, cover and cook on high for 4hours.

3. Put in the peas and cook for 30 minutes. Put lime juice and serve with cilantro and white rice.

4. Serve and enjoy!!!

# Classic Egg Salad Sandwich

Preparation Time: 10 minutes

Cook Time: 20 minutes

Total Time: 30 minutes

Serves: 4

**Ingredients:**

- 2 Scant Tbsp. mayonnaise
- 1 Tsp. yellow mustard
- Kosher salt
- 4 Eggs
- 4 Pieces white potato bread butter

**Cooking instructions:**

1. Put eggs in a saucepan, cover with cold water and boil over high heat. Take from heat, cover and let sit for 10 minutes.

2. Cool with cold water and ice cubes for 5 minutes. Crack eggs under cold running water. Keep aside. Whisk eggs in a bowl.

3. Put mayonnaise, mustard, salt and mix. Toast bread, butter and top two slices with half of egg mixture. Top wither served bread slices.

4. Serve and enjoy!!!

## Creamy Roasted Tomato Soup

Preparation Time: 10 minutes

Cook Time: 3 hour 30 minutes

Total Time: 3 hour 40 minutes

Serves: 4

**Ingredients:**

- 1½ Cup of chicken stock
- One baguette, thinly sliced
- Parmesan cheese, flaked
- Coarse salt
- Basil for garnish
- 3 Lbs. medium tomatoes, sliced in half crosswise
- 1 Tbsp. Italian seasoning
- ½ Cup of olive oil
- 4 Cloves garlic
- 1 Cup of heavy cream

**Cooking Instructions:**

1. Preheat your oven to 325ºF. Prepare the tomatoes and garlic on a large baking sheet and drizzle the oil over them.

2. Drizzle with the Italian seasoning, and a pinch of salt. Roast for 3 hours 30 minutes. Flip the tomatoes and the garlic.

3. Squeeze out of their skins to a blender and blend. Put in the cream and stock, and blend. Flip the soup to a medium pot and bring it to a simmer.

4. Toast the baguette and add a little oil and the parmesan flakes. Top the soup garnished with basil and with the parmesan toast.

5. Serve and enjoy!!!

# POULTRY RECIPES

## BBQ Chicken Salad

Preparation Time: 10 minutes

Cook Time: 10 minutes

Total Time: 20 minutes

Serves: 4

**Ingredients:**

- 2 White corn tortillas
- Cooking spray
- Kosher salt
- Chili powder
- Garlic salt
- 1/3 Cup of good quality BBQ sauce
- 1 Cup of corn kernels frozen and then thawed, grilled
- 2 Tbsp. rice wine vinegar
- Honey to taste
- ¼ Cup of fresh cilantro chopped
- Cotija cheese
- Sliced jalapeño pepper
- Juice of 1 lime
- 4 Cups of salad greens such as romaine iceberg
- 1 6Oz. grilled BBQ chicken breast sliced
- ½ Cup of canned cannellini beans rinsed and drained
- 2 Small tomatoes diced

**Cooking Instruction:**

1. Put the lettuce in a large bowl. Top with the sliced grilled chicken, cannellini beans, corn, tomato and cilantro.

2. Drizzle with cotija cheese and sliced jalapeño and keep aside. Place the corn tortillas on a baking sheet lined with aluminium foil.

3. Spray each side of the tortillas with cooking spray and drizzle each side with kosher salt, chili powder and garlic salt.

4. Put in a toaster oven and toast. Allow to cool, then cut into strips and drizzle over the salad.

5. Whisk the BBQ sauce, lime and rice wine vinegar in a small bowl. Add honey to taste. Top over the salad and mix.

6. Garnish with cilantro, cotija cheese and sliced jalapeño peppers.

7. Serve and enjoy!!!

# Cheesy Chicken and Broccoli Whole Wheat Pasta

Preparation Time: 10 minutes

Cook Time: 10 minutes

Total Time: 20 minutes

Serves: 4

**Ingredients:**

- 1 Tbsp. whole-grain mustard
- Kosher salt and freshly ground black pepper
- 1 ½ Cups shredded fontina cheese
- ½ Cup grated parmesan cheese plus more for garnishing
- 2 Cups shredded cooked chicken breast
- 8 Oz. DeLallo short whole wheat such as fusilli
- 4 Cups broccoli florets
- 2 Tbsp. butter
- 3 Tbsp. all-purpose flour
- 2 Cups low-fat milk

**Cooking Instructions:**

1. Cook pasta in salted water and properly drain pasta into a bowl and reserve the hot pasta water.

2. Put the broccoli in the pasta water and cook for about 3 minutes. Drain and keep aside. While pasta is cooking, make the cheese sauce.

3. Melt butter in a big sauce pan and mix in the flour over medium high heat. Cook while stirring for about 2 minutes.

4. Add milk and mix. Cook stir often, for about 5 minutes. Add in the mustard and spice with kosher salt and freshly ground black pepper.

5. Remove from the heat and put in the cheeses. Put the chicken breast, the whole wheat pasta and the broccoli and stir to mix.

6. Spice with more salt and pepper to taste and garnish with shredded parmesan cheese

7. Serve and enjoy!!!

## Chicken Piccata Pasta

Preparation Time: 10 minutes

Cook Time: 24 minutes

Total Time: 34 minutes

Serves: 4

**Ingredients:**

- 2 Tbsp. canola or extra virgin olive oil
- 1 Lbs. chicken breasts cubed
- 12 Button mushrooms sliced
- ¼ Cup of panko bread crumbs
- 1 Lbs. rotini pasta cooked and drained
- 1 Tbsp. fresh tarragon slivered
- 1 Tsp. pepper
- Salt to taste
- 5 Tbsp. butter 1 Tbsp. reserved
- ½ Cup of white wine
- 1 Cup of chicken broth
- Juice of 1 lemon
- 1 Cup of grape or cherry tomatoes
- ¼ Cup of capers

**Cooking Instructions:**

1. Heat a large skillet over medium-high heat and put 1 Tbsp. olive oil. Add chicken pieces and cook for 7 minutes.

2. Remove from pan and put remaining Tbsp. of olive oil. Sauté mushrooms for 5 minutes and spice with salt.

3. Remove mushrooms from skillet and reduce heat to medium. Put 4 Tbsp. butter and mix in wine and chicken broth and lemon juice.

4. Put tomatoes and capers and cook for 8 minutes. Heat a small skillet over medium heat and melt remaining Tbsp. butter. Put breadcrumbs, mix.

5. Cook for 3 minutes, stir frequently. Put pasta, tarragon, chicken and mushrooms in sauce and cook for 1 minute, tossing to dredge.

6. Top with 2 Tsp. of browned breadcrumbs. Serve and enjoy!!!

# Buffalo Chicken Grilled Cheese

Preparation Time: 10 minutes

Cook Time: 7 minutes

Total Time: 17 minutes

Serves: 4

**Ingredients:**

- 1 Cooked chicken breast shredded
- 1 Cup Frank's Red Hot Buffalo
- Wing Sauce
- 8 Slices jalapeño bread
- 4 Oz. Monterey Jack cheese sliced
- 4 Oz. blue cheese
- 4 Tbsp. butter

**Cooking Instructions:**

1. Mix together the shredded chicken breast and Frank's Red Hot sauce in a medium bowl.

2. Put ½ Tbsp. of butter on one side of each slice of the bread, and then put buttered sides together.

3. Put 1 oz. Of Monterey Jack on each bread stack, then put dollop of hot sauce slathered chicken breast and add 1 Oz. of blue cheese crumbles.

4. Put bread buttered side down in a fry pan over medium heat. Cover with a lid and allow cook for 4 minutes.

5. Minimize the heat to medium-low and transfer sandwich to the other side and cook for 3 minutes.

6. The second side will cook faster than the first so watch carefully. Divide in two. Serve and enjoy!!!

## Balsamic and Honey Chicken Skewers

Preparation Time: 10 minutes

Freezing Time: 2 hours

Cook Time: 45 minutes

Total Time: 2 hours 55minutes

Serves: 6

**Ingredients:**

- 1 Clove garlic minced
- 3 Tbsp. honey divided
- 1 Tsp. fresh rosemary minced,
- Kosher salt and freshly ground black pepper
- 1 Lbs. boneless skinless chicken breasts, about 2 breasts
- 2 Tbsp. balsamic vinegar
- 1 Tbsp. extra virgin olive oil

**Cooking Instructions:**

1. Collect 5 wooden skewers and put in a shallow plate with water for about 30minutes.Cut any extra fat from the chicken breasts.

2. Cut into chunks and keep aside. Whisk the balsamic vinegar, extra virgin olive oil, garlic, 1 Tbsp. honey and 1 Tsp. rosemary, a pinch of kosher salt.

3. Add freshly ground black pepper. Put the chunks of chicken breast. Refrigerate for about2 hours.

4. Preheat the grill to high. Arrange the chunks of chicken onto the wooden skewers. Spray the grill with non-stick cooking spray.

5. Reduce the heat to medium-high. Cook the chicken for about 5 minutes on each side, drizzle the chicken with the remaining honey.

6. Continue flipping for about 10 minutes. Allow to settle for about 3 minutes. Drizzle with more honey and fresh rosemary.

7. Serve and enjoy!!!

# Asian Glazed Orange Chicken

Preparation Time: 10 minutes

Cook Time: 20 minutes

Total Time: 30 minutes

Serves: 4

## Ingredients:

- ½ Cup of brown sugar
- ½ Cup of hoisin sauce
- 4 Cloves garlic minced or pressed
- 2 Heaping Tbsp. orange zest
- Inch knob ginger peeled and grated
- 8 Skinless boneless chicken thighs
- Kosher salt and freshly ground black pepper
- 1 Tbsp. olive oil
- 1 Cup of fresh squeezed orange juice from about 4 oranges
- 1 Cup of chicken broth
- 1 Tsp. sriracha sauce
- Cilantro leaves, sliced
- Orange for garnish

## Cooking Instructions:

1. Preheat oven to 350°F. Spice the chicken thighs with kosher salt and freshly ground black pepper. Heat the oil in a frying pan over medium heat.

2. Put half of the chicken thighs in the pan and cook both sides of the chicken. Flip to a plate and repeat with the remaining thighs.

3. Mix the remaining ingredients in a medium bowl. Put into the same pan and put the sauce over medium heat and cook.

4. Put the chicken back to the pan and bake in the oven for about 20 minutes. Remove the chicken from pan, flip to a serving plate, and reserve the glaze.

5. Cover the chicken with aluminium foil to keep warm. Cook the glaze over medium heat.

6. Sprinkle over the chicken and garnish with cilantro and sliced oranges.

7. Serve and enjoy!!!

# Chicken Nicoise Pasta Salad

Preparation Time: 10 minutes

Cook Time: 10 minutes

Total Time: 20 minutes

Serves: 4

## Ingredients:

- 1 Red bell pepper
- ¼ Cup of red onion
- ¼ Cup of capers
- 1/3 Cup of caesar salad dressing
- 1 Tsp. champagne vinegar
- Kosher salt and freshly ground black pepper
- ½ Lbs. fettuccine noodles
- 1 Cooked chicken breast sliced
- ½ Lbs. green beans
- ½ Cucumber

## Cooking Instructions:

1. Boil a big pot of water. Sprinkle a generous amount of salt and put fettuccine noodles. Cook and Strain noodles, reserving water in pot.

2. Rinse noodles and put aside to cool. Cut ends of green beans and put in hot noodle water. Drain after one minute then rinse in cold water and put aside.

3. Peel cucumber and red onion and thinly cut. Seed and core red bell pepper and thinly slice.

4. Mix fettuccine, green beans, cucumber, red bell pepper, red onion and capers separately on a serving plate.

5. Combine dressing with champagne vinegar and dress fettuccine noodles then spice with kosher salt and pepper.

6. Serve and enjoy!!!

# Chinese Chicken Salad with Sesame Dressing

Preparation Time: 10 minutes

Cook Time: 30 seconds

Total Time: 10 minutes 30 seconds

Serves: 2

**Ingredients:**

**For The Salad:**

- 2 Green onions chopped
- ¼ Cup of sliced almonds toasted lightly
- 1 Tbsp. sesame seeds
- 2 Cups of cooked fusilli pasta noodles cooled
- 12 3- Inch wonton skins sliced into ¼ strips
- ¼ Cup of canola oil for frying
- 4 Cups of chopped romaine lettuce
- 1 Chicken breast shredded

**For The Dressing:**

- 2 Tsp. light soy sauce
- 2 Tbsp. sesame seeds
- ½ Tsp. fresh ground pepper
- 1/8 Tbsp. kosher salt
- 1 ½ Tbsp. canola oil
- 6 Tbsp. seasoned rice vinegar
- 1 Tsp. sesame oil
- 1 ½ Tsp. sugar

**Cooking Instructions:**

1. Heat canola oil in a skillet over medium-high heat. When oil starts to boil, fry the wonton skins in batches of 7 strips for 30 seconds on both sides.

2. Take from the oil and drain on paper towels. Mix lettuce, chicken breast, green onion, almonds, and pasta in a big bowl.

3. Put the dressing ingredients in a jar with a lid and shake. Dress the lettuce mixture with 3 Tbsp. of sesame dressing and top with more sesame seeds, wonton strips.

4. Serve and enjoy!!!

# Chicken Caesar Salad

Preparation Time: 10 minutes

Cook Time: 30 seconds

Total Time: 10 minutes 30 seconds

Serves: 4

**Ingredients:**

- 1 Cup of croutons
- ½ Cup of grated Parmesan cheese
- 2 Large eggs coddled
- 1 Clove garlic pressed
- 4 Anchovy filets in oil roughly chopped
- Juice of ½ lemon
- 1 Tsp. Worcestershire sauce
- ¼ Tsp. dry mustard
- Kosher salt and freshly ground black pepper
- 1/3 Cup of extra virgin olive oil
- 10 Cups of romaine lettuce chopped into ½ Inch pieces
- 4 Cups of cooked shredded chicken breast
- 1 Cucumber sliced into coins

**Cooking Instructions:**

1. Arrange the coddled eggs by putting the eggs in warm water. Cook the eggs in boiling water with a slotted spoon then remove from heat.

2. Cover and allow for 30 seconds and dip into cold water. Break the eggs open and separate the eggs from the whites.

3. Put the eggs in a blender, and preserve the whites for another use. Put the pressed garlic, anchovy filets, dry mustard, salt, lemon juice, Worcestershire sauce, and pepper in the blender.

4. Blend on high. Slowly sprinkle the olive oil into the blender. Put in a small jar and put aside. Put the romaine lettuce, chicken breast and cucumber in a large bowl.

5. Put about 2/3 of the dressing and throw to coat. Put the croutons and Parmesan cheese, throw lightly and spice with more salt and pepper to taste.

6. Serve and enjoy!!!

# Chicken Divan Macaroni and Cheese

Preparation Time: 10 minutes

Cook Time: 41 minutes

Total Time: 51 minutes

Serves: 8

**Ingredients:**

- 4 Cups of 16 ounces Wisconsin Fontina Cheese, shredded
- ½ Cup of 2 Oz. Wisconsin
- Parmesan Cheese, grated
- 2 Cups of boneless skinless chicken breast, cooked and diced
- 1 Lbs. frozen broccoli spears thawed
- ½ Cup of panko bread crumbs
- 1 Lbs. elbow macaroni
- 5 Tbsp. butter divided
- 3 Tbsp. flour
- 1 Tbsp. curry powder
- 4 Cups of cold whole milk
- 1 Tsp. salt
- 1 Tsp. pepper

**Cooking Instructions:**

1. Preheat oven to 350°F. Cook macaroni and properly drain noodles and keep aside. Melt 4 Tbsp. butter over medium-high heat in big saucepan.

2. Put flour and curry powder and mix well, cook for about 1 minute. Put cold milk and mix. Boil mixture and continue to mix occasionally as mixture becomes thick, about 5 minutes.

3. Put salt and pepper, put cheeses and mix. Put chicken, broccoli and cooked macaroni to cheese mixture, fold to coat and cook on stovetop over medium heat for about5 minutes.

4. Put mixture into buttered baking dish. Melt remaining 1 Tbsp. Butter, put bread crumbs and mix.

5. Top macaroni mixtures with buttered bread crumbs and bake 25 minutes. Remove from oven, let rest 5 minutes.

6. Serves and enjoy!!!

# FISH & SEAFOOD RECIPES

## Crab Salad Sweet Potato Chip Bites

Preparation Time: 15 minutes

Total Time: 15 minutes

Serves: 24

**Ingredients:**

- 1 Cup of lump crab meat about 4 ounces
- 1/3 Cup of celery chopped fine
- 2 Tbsp. shallots minced
- ½ Tsp. dried thyme
- 4 Tbsp. crémé fraiche
- 1 Tsp. fresh lemon juice
- 1 Cup of grated Swiss cheese
- Kosher salt and fresh ground pepper
- 2 Tbsp. chives chopped
- 3 Cups of sweet potato chips

**Cooking Instructions:**

1. Combine lump crab meat with chopped celery, shallots, crémé fraiche and lemon juice.

2. Put thyme and Swiss cheese and spice with kosher salt and pepper.

3. Put about 1 Tbsp. of crab mixture on each chip and garnish with chopped chives.

4. Serve and enjoy!!!

# Citrus Shrimp and Avocado Salad

Preparation Time: 10 minutes

Cook Time: 10 minutes

Serves: 4

**Ingredients:**

- 1 Avocado sliced
- 1 Shallot minced
- 4 Oz. toasted sliced almonds
- Kosher salt and freshly ground black pepper
- 1 Lbs. medium Pan-Seared citrus Shrimp
- 8 Cups of greens such as arugula spinach
- Fruity extra virgin olive oil
- Juice of ½ lemon

**Cooking Instructions:**

1. Prepare the recipe for the Pan-Seared Citrus Shrimp. In a large bowl, toss the shrimp with the salad greens.

2. Sprinkle with olive oil, put some of the sauce remaining from the shrimp with a generous squeeze of citrus, and toss to dredge.

3. Put the avocado, shallots and sliced almonds and then spice with kosher salt and freshly ground black pepper.

4. Serve and enjoy!!!

# Baked Salmon with Creme Fraiche

Preparation Time: 10 minutes

Cook Time: 15 minutes

Total Time: 25 minutes

Serves: 6

**Ingredients:**

- ½ Cup of white wine
- 8 Oz. Crème fraiche
- 2 Tbsp. minced shallot
- 2 Tbsp. fresh dill
- 6 6-Oz. salmon filets
- 1/8 Tbsp. kosher salt
- 1/8 Tsp. freshly ground black pepper
- 1 Lemon, sliced

**Cooking Instructions:**

1. Preheat the oven to 425°F. Spice the salmon with the salt and pepper. Put the salmon, skin side down, in a baking dish.

2. Top the salmon with the lemon slices and put the wine to the dish. Bake for about 15 minutes.

3. Combine the crème fraiche, minced shallot, and dill in a medium bowl. Top over each of the salmon filets.

4. Serve and enjoy!!!

# Crab and Shrimp Seafood Cobb Salad

Preparation Time: 10 minutes

Total Time: 10 minutes

Serves: 4

**Ingredients:**

- 4 Cocktail tomatoes diced
- 2 Hard-boiled eggs diced
- 2 Oz. crumbled blue cheese
- 1 Avocado sliced
- 4 Slices thick cut bacon diced
- 6 Cups of sliced romaine lettuce
- ¼ Lbs. bay shrimp
- ¼ Lbs. snow crab meat

**For the Market Street Red Wine Vinaigrette:**

- 1 Tbsp. chopped fresh Italian parsley
- 1 Tbsp. crushed black peppercorns
- ½ kosher salt
- ½ Cup of canola oil
- ½ Cup of red wine vinegar
- 2 Tbsp. minced shallots

**Cooking Instructions:**

1. Cook the diced bacon in a big sauce pan, drain on a paper towel and let cool. In the bottom of a big bowl, put the romaine lettuce.

2. Add the salad toppings in rows on top of the lettuce. Serve with ¼ cup of the red wine vinaigrette dressing and refrigerate the rest.

3. For the market street red wine vinaigrette, put the ingredients in a large bowl and mix together.

4. Serve and enjoy!!!

# Crab and Avocado Grilled Cheese

Preparation Time: 10 minutes

Cook Time: 7 minutes

Total Time: 17 minutes

Serves: 4

**Ingredients:**

- 8 Oz. fresh snow crab meat
- 2 Tbsp. butter
- 4 Slices sourdough bread
- 2 Slices Havarti cheese
- ½ Avocado pitted and sliced

**Cooking Instructions:**

1. Spread ½ Tbsp. of butter on one side of each slice of the bread, and then stick buttered sides together.

2. Slice the Havarti slices into two and layer 1 half slice on top of each bread stack, and then add a few slices of avocado.

3. Add half of the snow crab on each bread stack plus the remaining Havarti cheese slices. Put bread buttered side down in a fry pan over medium heat.

4. Cover and cook for 4 minutes. Reduce the heat to medium-low and flip sandwich to the other side and cook for 3 minutes.

5. The second side will cook faster than the first so watch carefully. Cut into two.

6. Serve and enjoy!!!

# Shrimp Cocktail

Preparation Time: 10 minutes

Thawing Time: 15 minutes

Total Time: 25 minutes

Serves: 5

Calories: 188 kcal

**Ingredients:**

- 1 Lbs. Simple Truth Extra Large, Peeled and Deveined Cooked Shrimp
- ½ Cup of Kroger Chilli Sauce
- ½ Lemon
- 2 Tsp. prepared hot horseradish
- ½ Tsp. Worcestershire sauce
- ½ Tsp. ground mustard

**Cooking Instructions:**

1. Thaw the shrimp in the refrigerator overnight and rinse with cold water, then set aside.

2. Combine the chilli sauce with 1 Tbsp. of fresh lemon juice, the horseradish, Worcestershire sauce and ground mustard in a small bowl. Chop the rest of the lemon into sizes.

3. Top a platter with crushed ice cubes, the shrimp and lemon wedges and with the cocktail sauce on the side.

4. Serve and enjoy!!!

# Blackened Seafood Pasta

Preparation Time: 10 minutes

Cook Time: 10 minutes

Total Time: 20 minutes

Serves: 4

**Ingredients:**

- 1 Lbs. chorizo sausages cut into ½ inch pieces
- 1 Large red bell pepper cut into ½ inch dice
- 2 Tomatoes seeded and cut into ½ inch dice
- ¾ Cup of heavy cream
- 5 Green onions chopped
- 1 Lbs. fettuccine
- 1 Lbs. sea scallops cut in half
- 1 Lbs. medium size white shrimp shelled and deveined
- 3 Tbsp. blackening seasoning
- 2 Tbsp. extra virgin olive oil divided
- 4 Tbsp. butter divided

**Cooking Instructions:**

1. Cook fettuccine in big pot of water and properly drain and keep aside. Combine sea scallops and shrimp in big bowl with blackening seasoning and keep aside.

2. Heat 1 Tbsp. olive oil plus 1 Tbsp. butter in large frying pan over medium high heat. Put chorizo and cook for 7 minutes.

3. Take chorizo from pan, put remaining Tbsp. of oil and sea scallops and shrimp and cook for about 2 minutes before flipping. Cook for another 2 minutes.

4. Put bell pepper, tomatoes and cooked chorizo slices and cook for another 4 minutes, stir often.

5. Put in cream and 3 Tbsp. of butter and cook for 2 minutes. Put cooked fettuccine and throw to coat.

6. Top immediately garnished with the chopped green onions.

7. Serve and enjoy!!!

# Chicken, Sausage and Shrimp Jambalaya

Preparation Time: 10 minutes

Cook Time: 34 minutes

Total Time: 44 minutes

Serves: 4

**Ingredients:**

- 3 Tbsp. Creole seasoning
- 2 Bay leaves
- 1 Tbsp. hot sauce
- 2 ½ Cups of long grain rice
- 1 16- Oz. bag medium shrimp deveined and shelled
- 1 Cup of frozen okra
- Kosher salt to taste
- 3 Green onions chopped
- 4 Tbsp. butter
- 1 Tbsp. vegetable oil
- 2 Skinless boneless chicken breasts, cubed
- 1 Lbs. andouille sausage sliced
- 2 Ribs celery chopped
- 1 Medium yellow onion chopped
- 1 Green bell pepper seeded and chopped
- 3 Cloves garlic peeled and minced
- 1 28- Oz. can crushed tomatoes
- 3 Cups of chicken stock 24 ounces

**Cooking Instructions:**

1. Dissolve 2 Tbsp. butter and vegetable oil in big skillet over medium high heat. Put chicken breasts and andouille sausages slice.

2. Cook for 6minutes, stir occasionally. Remove from pan and keep aside. Lower heat to medium, put the additional 2 Tbsp. of butter and put the celery, onion, bell pepper and garlic.

3. Cook for 8 minutes. Put crushed tomatoes, chicken stock, creole seasoning, bay leaves and hot sauce.

4. Cook for 5 minutes then put rice and cook for about 15 minutes. Put chicken and sausage back to pan with shrimp and the okra and cook.

5. Spice with kosher salt to taste and garnish with green onions.

6. Serve and enjoy!!!

# Classic Shrimp Macaroni Salad

Preparation Time: 10 minutes

Freezing Time: 1 hour

Total Time: 1 hour 10minutes

Serves: 4

**Ingredients:**

- 3 Cups of uncooked medium shell pasta
- 1 Lbs. bay salad shrimp
- 2 Ribs celery chopped
- 3 Green onions chopped
- 10 Sweet pickles chopped
- 3 Hard-boiled eggs chopped
- 1 Cup of mayonnaise
- 8 Tbsp. of pickle juice
- Kosher salt and freshly ground black pepper

**Cooking Instructions:**

1. Cook the macaroni shells properly, rinse under cold water, drain and allow cool.

2. Put the pasta to a big bowl with the bay salad shrimp, celery, green onions, pickles, and chopped eggs.

3. Combine the mayonnaise to a small bowl with the pickle juice and spice with kosher salt and freshly ground black pepper. Put more pickle juice.

4. Top the dressing over the macaroni and toss to coat. Spice with more kosher salt and pepper. Make the salad ahead of time and refrigerate for at least one hour.

5. Serve and enjoy!!!

## Maple Oatmeal with Sweet Potato

Preparation Time: 10 minutes

Cook Time: 1 minute 30 seconds

Total Time: 11 minutes 30 seconds

Serves: 4

**Ingredients:**

- ½ Cup of oatmeal old fashioned
- 2/3 Cup of non-fat milk
- Pinch of salt
- 1/3 Cup of cooked sweet potato mashed
- 2 Tsp. brown sugar
- Pumpkin pie spice
- Maple syrup
- Chopped almonds

**Cooking Instructions:**

1. Combine the oats, milk, salt and sweet potato in a microwave safe bowl and cook on high for 1 minute 30 seconds.

2. Remove from the microwave and drizzle with brown sugar and a pinch of pumpkin pie spice and mix.

3. Sprinkle with maple syrup, put a small handful of chopped almonds and put more milk.

4. Serve and enjoy!!!

# BEANS, RICE & GRAIN RECIPES

## Greek White Bean Soup with Orange Slices

Preparation Time: 15 minutes

Cook Time: 30 minutes

Total Time: 45 minutes

Serves: 8

### Ingredients:

- 4 15-Oz. cans cannellini white beans
- 2 Cups of water
- 4 Large carrots, sliced thin
- 5 Celery sticks, sliced thin
- 1 Large onion, sliced thin
- 1 Bay leaf
- 3 Slices orange
- 2 Tbsp. tomato paste
- 1 Cup of extra virgin olive oil
- ½ Tsp. dried oregano

### Cooking Instructions:

1. Cook carrots, onions and celery in olive oil on medium heat.
2. Put oregano and bay leaf.
3. Put orange slices and tomato paste. Cook for 2 minutes
4. Put Cannellini beans, 2 cans drained, 2 cans with liquid. Put 2 cups water.
5. Cook for 40 minutes, stir often.
6. Serve and enjoy!!!

## Oatmeal Recipe for Steel Cut Oats

Preparation Time: 10 minutes

Cook Time: 3 minutes

Total Time: 13 minutes

Serves: 4

### Ingredients:

- 2 Cups of water
- 1 Cup of Almond Breeze almond milk Vanilla
- 1 Cup of steel cut oats
- 1 Cinnamon stick
- 1 Generous pinch of kosher salt

### Cooking Instructions:

1. Put the oatmeal and the liquid ratios that match to the pot of your Instant Pot with the cinnamon stick and kosher salt.

2. Press the manual setting and set the cooking time for 3 minutes on high. Put toppings of your choice with additional almond milk to taste.

3. Serve and enjoy!!!

# Beans and Greens over Polenta

Preparation Time: 15 minutes

Cook Time: 60 minutes

Total Time: 75 minutes

Serves: 8

**Ingredients:**

- 1 Bunch Swiss chard, washed and chopped
- 2 Cans black eyed peas, drained
- 1 Tbsp. tomato paste
- Juice of 1 lemon
- Salt and pepper, to taste
- 1 Cup of extra virgin olive oil
- ½ Onion, chopped
- ½ Cup of chopped parsley
- ½ Cup of chopped dill

**For Polenta:**

- ¼ Cup soy, almond or regular milk
- 2 Tbsp. extra virgin olive oil
- Salt and pepper, to taste
- 4 Cups water or vegetable broth
- 1 Cup cornmeal
- 1 Clove garlic, minced

**Cooking Instructions**

1. For the Beans and Greens, cook the onion in the olive oil on medium heat in a pot for about 2 minutes, put parsley and dill and cook for 2 minutes.

2. Put the Swiss chard and cook for 2 minutes. Put the beans, tomato paste, lemon juice, and seasoning. Simmer for 30minutes.

3. For the Polenta, boil the water in a small pot. Put the cornmeal in and lower the heat to medium low. Cook the polenta for 15 minutes stir often.

4. Put milk, garlic, olive oil, salt and pepper, and mix well. Top the polenta with beans and greens.

5. Serve and enjoy!!!

## Teriyaki Chicken Rice Bowls

Preparation Time: 10 minutes

Cook Time: 4 minutes

Total Time: 14 minutes

Serves: 4

**Ingredients:**

- 4 Green onions roughly chopped
- 1 Cup of snap peas
- 2 Cups of napa cabbage roughly chopped
- Sesame seeds
- 4 Cups of cooked white rice
- 4 cups of shredded slow cooker teriyaki chicken
- 1½ Tbsp. canola oil
- 1 Tbsp. grated and peeled fresh ginger
- 2 Carrots peeled and sliced
- 1 Red bell pepper thinly sliced

**Cooking Instructions:**

1. Slice the chicken and reserve 1cup of the sauce. Heat a large skillet over high heat, put the canola oil and cook for about30 seconds.

2. Put the ginger and cook, for about 30 seconds, stir occasionally. Put in the reserved teriyaki sauce and allow boil.

3. Put the carrots, bell pepper and snap peas and stir-fry for 3 minutes. Put the reserved chicken and the cabbage and cook.

4. Top the chicken over rice, drizzle with sesame seeds and chopped green onion.

5. Serve and enjoy!!!

# Sweet Corn, Gouda and Farro Risotto

Preparation Time: 10 minutes

Cook Time: 48 minutes

Total Time: 58 minutes

Serves: 4

## Ingredients:

- ¾ Cup of organic faro soaked in water overnight in the refrigerator
- 4 Cups of vegetable broth
- 2 Tbsp. extra virgin olive oil
- 1 Medium yellow onion small diced
- 1 Small carrot small diced
- 1 Stick celery small diced
- 2 Tbsp. crushed garlic
- 2 Ears sweet corn kernels removed
- 1 Cup of white wine
- 1 Cup of gouda cheese shredded
- ¼ Cup of butter
- ¼ Cup of Italian flat leaf parsley chopped
- Kosher salt and freshly ground pepper to taste

## Cooking Instructions:

1. Drain the faro, and keep aside. Bring the broth to a simmer in a medium saucepan. In another skillet, heat the oil over medium heat.

2. Put the onion, carrots, celery and garlic and cook. Put the sweet corn and mix. Put the wine and cook.

3. Put the faro and cook for 3minutes and stir occasionally. Put the broth ½ cups at a time, continue to stir, add the remaining gradually, about45 minutes.

4. Take the faro from the heat and stir in the butter, gouda and parsley. Spice with salt and pepper to taste.

5. Serve and enjoy!!!

# Chicken and Rice Casserole

Preparation Time: 10 minutes

Cook Time: 25 minutes

Total Time: 35 minutes

Serves: 4

**Ingredients:**

- 3 Tbsp. Simple Truth butter
- 1 Medium onion, chopped
- 2 Cloves garlic, minced or pressed
- 2 Tsp. kosher salt
- 1 Tsp. Private Selection dried thyme
- 1 ½ Cups of long grain white rice
- 1 Carrot, diced
- 3 Cups of Simple Truth chicken broth
- 1 12-Oz. can evaporated milk
- 1 Lbs. skinless, boneless chicken
- ½ Tsp. freshly ground black pepper
- 1 10-Oz. bag frozen peas
- 1 Cup of shredded cheddar cheese

**Cooking Instructions:**

1. Melt the butter in a large skillet over medium to medium-high heat. Put the onion, garlic, 1 Tsp. of salt and thyme. Cook, about 7 minutes, stir often.

2. Put the rice and carrot and cook for 3minutes. Put the chicken broth and evaporated milk and add the chicken, the remaining salt and the black pepper.

3. Bring to a boil then reduce to a simmer. Stir and cover then cook for about 15 minutes, and stir.

4. Put in the peas and put more vegetable broth. Drizzle with the cheese and cover with the lid to dissolve the cheese.

5. Serve and enjoy!!!

# Black Eyed Beans and Avocado Salad Crete

Preparation Time: 10 minutes

Cook Time: 30 minutes

Total Time: 40 minutes

Serves: 8

**Ingredients:**

- 4 Cups of water
- 1 Lbs. black eyed beans, soaked overnight
- 3 Scallions, chopped
- 2 Tomatoes cut into cubes
- ½ Cup of parsley, chopped
- 2 Avocados, cut into small pieces
- ½ Cup of fresh lemon juice
- ½ Cup of extra virgin olive oil
- Salt and pepper, to taste

**Cooking Instructions:**

1. Strain and rinse soaked beans. Boil beans and 4 cups of water. Drain into a colander.

2. Combine the scallions, tomatoes, parsley, avocados and the beans in a large salad bowl.

3. Shake lemon juice and olive oil in a jar. Put this to the bowl. Toss well. Salt and pepper to taste.

4. Serve and enjoy!!!

# Fresh Tomato and Ricotta Whole Wheat Pasta

Preparation Time: 10 minutes

Cook Time: 9 minutes

Total Time: 19 minutes

Serves: 4

**Ingredients:**

- 8 Oz. whole wheat short pasta
- ⅓ Cup of extra virgin olive oil
- Tomatoes, quartered
- Kosher salt and freshly ground black pepper
- 2 Cups of fresh spinach leaves
- ⅓ Cup of fresh basil slivered
- ½ Cup of freshly grated Parmesan cheese
- 1 Cup of fresh ricotta cheese

**Cooking Instructions:**

1. Cook the whole wheat pasta and properly Strain and remaining ¼ cup of the pasta water.

2. Heat the olive oil in a big sauté pan over medium heat. When hot, put the minced garlic and reduce heat to medium-low. Cook for about 5minutes.

3. Put the tomatoes and season with kosher salt and freshly cracked black pepper. Cook for 3 minutes.

4. Put the drained hot pasta in the tomatoes with the fresh spinach. Toss and cook.

5. Put the fresh basil leaves, grated parmesan cheese and more kosher salt and pepper to taste.

6. If the pasta is dry, sprinkle more olive oil. Top with dollops of fresh ricotta, sprinkle with more olive oil

7. Serve and enjoy!!!

# Lemon Rice

Preparation Time: 5 minutes

Cook Time: 20 minutes

Total Time: 25 minutes

Serves: 3

**Ingredients:**

- Zest and juice of 1 lemon
- 1 Cup of white rice
- 1 Tbsp. butter
- 1 Tsp. kosher salt
- 1 Tbsp. minced Italian parsley

**Cooking Instructions:**

1. Bring 1 ¾ cups of water to boil in a saucepan with a fitted lid. Put the lemon zest, lemon juice, rice, butter and salt, stir then reduce to boil and cover.

2. Cook for 20 minutes, then remove from the heat and fuzz with a fork. Put a kitchen towel over the pot and, put back the lid, and allow for 10minutes.

3. Fuzz with a fork and spice with more kosher salt to taste and put in the minced parsley.

4. Serve and enjoy!!!

# DESSERT RECIPES

## Spring Fever and Strawberry Banana Milkshake

Preparation Time: 2 minutes

Total Time: 2 minutes

### Ingredients:

- 3 Cups of vanilla ice cream
- ½ Cup of milk
- 2 Ripe bananas
- 8 Large strawberries sliced

### Cooking Instructions:

1. Put all the ingredients in a blender. Blend on high, adding more milk.

2. Serve and enjoy!!!

# Raspberry Peach Hand Pies

Preparation Time: 10 minutes

Cook Time: 25 minutes

Total Time: 35 minutes

Serves: 4

**Ingredients:**

- 1 Tbsp. butter
- 1 Tsp. almond extract
- 3 Refrigerated pie crusts 1½ boxes
- 1 Tbsp. milk
- 1 Tbsp. cream
- 5 Large peaches
- 8 Oz. fresh raspberries
- ½ Cup of granulated sugar
- ¼ Cup of tapioca or corn starch

**Cooking Instructions:**

1. Preheat the oven to 350°F. Peel the skins from the peaches and remove the pits. Chop into thick slices and combine with the raspberries in a big bowl.

2. Put sugar, tapioca, butter and almond extract and coat. Spread out the pie crusts and use a bowl about 6 inches across to chop the crust into smaller pieces.

3. Scoop 1/3 cup of the raspberries and peach mixture onto the cut discs to one side of the disc, leaving the edges clear.

4. Brush the edges of the circles with water, fold in half and fold the edges with the tines of a fork. Move the hand pies to a baking sheet linked with parchment paper.

5. Combine the milk and cream together and brush the tops of each pie with it and sprinkle with sugar. Bake for 25 minutes.

6. Serve and enjoy!!!

# Pumpkin Chocolate Chip Cookies

Preparation time: 10 minutes

Cook Time: 20 minutes

Total Time: 30 minutes

Serves: 4

**Ingredients:**

- 3 Cups of granulated sugar
- 1 29 Oz. can pure pumpkin
- 1½ Tsp. baking soda
- 1 Tsp. kosher salt
- 5 Cup of all-purpose flour
- 1 12 Oz. bag semi-sweet chocolate chips
- 1 Cup of butter melted
- 1 Tbsp. vanilla
- 2 Eggs
- 4 Tbsp. pumpkin pie spice
- 6 Tsp. baking powder

**Cooking Instructions:**

1. Preheat the oven to 375°F. Combine the sugar, pumpkin, melted butter and vanilla in the bowl of a stand mixer and mix.

2. Put the eggs and whisk for 2 minutes. Mix the pumpkin pie spice, baking powder, baking soda and kosher salt in a small bowl.

3. Add in the wet ingredients and combine. Add in 2 cups of the flour, then 2 more cups and then the last cup.

4. Put the chocolate chips and combine. Spread a baking sheet with parchment paper. Put 1 Tbsp. rounded scoops of the cookie dough on the sheet about 2 inches apart.

5. Bake cookies for 15 minutes. Set aside rest on cookie sheet for 3 minutes then flip to a rack to cool completely.

6. Serve and enjoy!!!

# Dreamy Creamy Mango Pops

Preparation time: 10 minutes

Freezing Time: 6 hours 30 minutes

Total Time: 6 hours 40 minutes

Serves: 8

**Ingredients:**

- Hint of Honey Vanilla divided
- ½ Cup of non-fat Greek vanilla flavoured yogurt
- 1 Tbsp. sugar or more to taste
- 4 Mangoes pitted and peeled
- 1¼ Cup of Almond Breeze Almond milk

**Cooking Instructions:**

1. Put 3 mangoes chopped, into a blender with ¾ cup almond milk, yogurt and sugar to taste and blend for 1 minute.

2. Chop the other mango into small sizes and put a few pieces in the bottoms of the Popsicle mould.

3. Put the blended mango mixture into the bottom 1/3 of the mould and freeze for about an hour.

4. Put a few more chunks of chopped mango to the middle 1/3 of the mould and fill the moulds to 2/3 full with the remaining ½ cup of the almond milk.

5. Put in your sticks and then freeze for another 30 minutes. Top with the rest of the mango mix and mango chunks. Freeze for at least 5 hours.

6. Serve and enjoy!!!

# Snicker doodles with White Chocolate Chips

Preparation time: 10 minutes

Cook Time: 12 minutes

Total Time: 22 minutes

Serves: 4

## Ingredients:

- 2¾ Cups of flour
- ¾ Cup of white chocolate chips
- 1½ Cup of sugar
- 2 Eggs
- 2 Tsp. cream of tartar
- 1 Tsp. soda
- ½ Tsp. salt
- 1 Recipe cinnamon sugar
- ⅛ Cup of sugar
- ½ Tbsp. cinnamon
- 1 Cup of butter-flavoured shortening

## Cooking Instructions:

1. Preheat oven to 375°F. Put all ingredients except the chocolate chips into a big bowl and mix with a standing mixer.

2. Put in chocolate chips and mix. Scoop 2 Tbsp. portions and roll dough into balls. Dip in cinnamon sugar mixture.

3. Add 6 to a lightly greased cookie sheet. Bake for about 12 minutes. Remove from sheet and cool.

4. Serve and enjoy!!!

## Shortcut Pie Dough Sugar Cookies

Preparation time: 10 minutes

Cook Time: 12 minutes

Total Time: 22 minutes

Serves: 12

**Ingredients:**

- ¾ Tsp. almond extract
- Decorative sugars
- 1 Roll refrigerator pie dough
- 1 Tbsp. melted butter

**Cooking Instructions:**

1. Preheat oven to 350ºF. Line a baking sheet with parchment paper. Roll pie dough into a ball and roll out to ¼ thick.

2. Cut dough with cookie cutters and put on the baking sheet. Put almond extract to melted butter and brush dough with butter.

3. Top generously with decorative sugars and bake for about 12 minutes. Remove from oven and cool for 10 minutes.

3. Serve and enjoy!!!

# Raspberries and Cream

Preparation Time: 15 minutes

Total Time: 15 minutes

## Ingredients:

- 2 Cups of whipping cream
- ¼ Cup of confectioners' sugar powdered sugar
- 1 Tsp. vanilla extract
- 2 Cups of Driscoll's raspberries 12 ounce package
- 2 Tbsp. granulated sugar

## Cooking Instructions:

1. Blend 1½ cups of the Driscoll's raspberries in a blender with the 2 Tbsp. of granulated sugar.

2. Add the cream, confectioners' sugar and vanilla extract in a big bowl. Mix with an electric hand mixer.

3. Gently fold in ¾ of the blended raspberries into the whipped cream mixture, leaving visible swirls. Fold in the rest of the puree.

4. Spoon the fool into 6 glass cups. Top with additional raspberries.

5. Serve and enjoy!!!

# Peach Pie Smoothie

Preparation Time: 10 minutes

Total Time: 10 minutes

Serves: 2

**Ingredients:**

- 1 Cup of ice cubes
- 1 Tbsp. honey
- 1 Tsp. almond extract
- 2 Cups of Almond Breeze Almond milk
- 2 Peaches peeled, pitted and sliced
- 1 Banana

**Cooking Instructions:**

1. Pour the almond milk into the blender.

2. Put the peaches, banana, ice cubes, honey and almond extract into the blender and blend. Garnish with peach slices.

3. Serve and enjoy!!!

## Apple and Oatmeal Rice Krispie Treats

Preparation Time: 10 minutes

Cook Time: 15 minutes

Total time: 25 minutes

Serves: 4

**Ingredients:**

- 10 Oz. bag mini marshmallows
- 2 Tbsp. butter
- 1 Tsp. vanilla
- 1 Tbsp. cinnamon
- 1 Tsp. nutmeg
- 1½ Cup of diced dried apple
- 2 Cups of quick oats
- 4 Cups of Rice Krispie cereal
- Caramel sauce

**Cooking Instructions:**

1. Melt butter over low heat in big saucepan. Put the marshmallows and mix. Remove from heat and put the vanilla, cinnamon and nutmeg and combine.

2. Mix together the dried apple, oatmeal and Rice Krispie cereal in a big bowl. Put the melted marshmallow mixture and stir well.

3. Grease your fingers with butter and press mixture into a buttered 8 X 8-inch pan. Pat well to compress.

4. Sprinkle with caramel sauce. Leave to cool for about 15 minutes and cut into squares.

5. Serve and enjoy!!!

# Strawberry and Quinoa Parfait

Preparation Time: 10 minutes

Total Time: 10 minutes

Serves: 3

**Ingredients:**

- 1 cup vanilla
- 2 Tbsp. honey
- 6 Strawberries stemmed and quartered
- ¼ Cup cooked quinoa
- 2 Tbsp. sliced almonds
- Fresh mint leaves for garnish

**Cooking Instructions:**

1. Combine the Greek yogurt and honey together in a bowl. Spoon ⅓ of the yogurt mixture into a glass.

2. Top with ⅓ of the quartered strawberries and ⅓ of the quinoa. Drizzle with a few almonds slices.

3. Do same with the remaining yogurt, quinoa, strawberries and almonds to make three.

4. Garnish with fresh mint leaves and sprinkle with additional honey.

5. Serve and enjoy!!!

# SNACK RECIPES

## Currant Cookies

Preparation Time: 10 minutes

Cook Time: 15 minutes

Total Time: 25 minutes

Serves: 4

**Ingredients:**

- ¼ Cup of milk
- 1 Cup of butter softened
- 3 Cups of rolled oats
- 1 Cup of sugar
- ¾ Cup of flour
- 1 Tsp. baking soda
- ½ Tsp. ground cloves
- ½ Tsp. cinnamon
- ½ Cup of currants

**Cooking Instructions:**

1. Preheat oven to 350ºF. Using hand mixer, put the butter and sugar, and then put the oats and mix.

2. Blend in flour, soda, cloves and cinnamon. Stir in currants and milk, and combine.

3. Mould into balls and put on a baking sheet lined with parchment paper. Bake for15 minutes. Remove and allow cool.

4. Serve and enjoy!!!

# Pull-Apart Cinnamon Pecan Rolls

Preparation Time: 8 hours

Cook Time: 30 minutes

Total Time: 8 hours 30 minutes

## Ingredients:

- 1 Cup of chopped pecans
- 20 Frozen dinner rolls
- 1 3.5 Oz. package butterscotch pudding not instant
- 10 Tbsp. butter
- 1 Cup of brown sugar
- 1 ½ Tbsp. McCormick Ground Cinnamon

## Cooking Instructions:

1. Spray the bottom and sides of a non-stick Bundt pan generously with cooking or spray. Drizzle nuts on the bottom of the pan and on the sides.

2. Put the rolls on top of the nuts. Drizzle rolls evenly with the butterscotch pudding. Dissolve the butter.

3. Add the brown sugar and cinnamon then drizzle over the rolls. Set the pan out in a non-drifty place for 8 hours.

4. For a faster rise method, put the prepared Bundt pan in the oven at 200°F for 1 hour. Preheat the oven to 350°F.

5. Bake the rolls for 30 minutes. Flip out the rolls from the Bundt pan

6. Serve and enjoy!!!

# Apple and Blueberry Crumble

Preparation Time: 10 minutes

Cook Time: 45 minutes

Total Time: 55 minutes

Serves: 4

**Ingredients:**

- 1 Tbsp. butter
- ½ Cup of quick oats
- 1 Cup of pecans coarsely chopped
- 6 Tbsp. butter
- ¼ Cup of brown sugar
- Pinch of kosher salt
- 1 Tsp. cinnamon
- 4 Gala apples sliced
- 1 Cup of blueberries
- 1 Lemon juiced
- 3 Tbsp. flour
- ½ Cup of sugar
- 1 Tbsp. cinnamon

**Cooking Instructions:**

1. Preheat oven to 350°F. Prepare a baking dish with butter. Put sliced apples to a large bowl and drizzle with lemon juice.

2. Put sugar, flour, cinnamon and toss to dredge. Put blueberries and toss lightly. Flip mixture to baking dish.

3. Mix oatmeal, brown sugar, pecans, cinnamon, salt and butter in a medium size bowl and combine together with fingers to form clumps of oatmeal mixture.

4. Top apple mixture with oatmeal mixture. Bake for 45 minutes. Serve hot with ice cream.

5. Serve and enjoy!!!

# Double Chocolate Zucchini Bread

Preparation Time: 10 minutes

Cook Time: 1 hour

Cool Time: 30 minutes

Total Time: 1 hour 40 minutes

Serves: 1

**Ingredients:**

- 3 Oz. cream cheese
- 1 ½ Cup of sugar
- 2 Eggs
- 1/3 Cup of canola oil
- 2 Cups of all-purpose flour
- ¼ Cup of cocoa powder
- 1 Tsp. baking powder
- 1 Tsp. baking soda
- 1 Tsp. vanilla
- ¾ Tbsp. salt
- 2 Cups of grated zucchini
- 1 Cup of pecans chopped
- 1 Cup of semi-sweet chocolate chips

**Cooking Instructions:**

1. Preheat the oven to 350°F. Spray a baking pan with cooking spray. Whisk the cream cheese and sugar with an electric mixer.

2. Put the eggs one at a time and blend, scrape the sides and bottom of the bowl. Whisk in the canola oil and the vanilla.

3. Filter the flour, cocoa powder, baking powder, baking soda and salt in another bowl. Put the flour mixture in the cream cheese mixture and blend well.

4. Whisk in the pecans, zucchini and chocolate morsels and put into the prepared pan. Bake for 65 minutes.

5. Cool for 30 minutes and then take from the pan. Serve and enjoy!!!

# Chocolate Cream Pie

Preparation Time: 10 minutes

Freezing Time: 2 hours

Total Time: 2 hours 10 minutes

Serves: 4

**Ingredients:**

**For the filling:**

- 2 Cups of milk
- 2 Oz. chopped bittersweet chocolate
- ½ Tsp. vanilla
- ½ Cup of granulated sugar
- 3 Tbsp. corn starch sifted
- 4 Tbsp. Unsweetened Cocoa powder sifted

**Toppings:**

- Chocolate shavings
- Sweetened whipped cream
- 1 9-Inch pie shell, cooked and cooled

**Cooking Instructions:**

1. Combine sugar, corn starch and cocoa powder together in a small pot. Mix in milk and put over medium heat.

2. When hot and thick take from heat and mix in chopped chocolate and vanilla. Flip into pie plate and cover with plastic wrap.

3. Make sure you put the plastic wrap directly on the filling. Refrigerate for 2hours.

4. Slice pie into 8 pieces and top with dollops of cream and chocolate shavings.

5. Serve and enjoy!!!

# Dark Chocolate Brownies Plus Friday Faves

Preparation Time: 10 minutes

Cook Time: 45 minutes

Total Time: 55 minutes

Serves: 4

**Ingredients:**

- 7 Oz. unsweetened chocolate coarsely chopped
- ¾ Cup of butter
- ¼ Cup of water
- 1 Cup of granulated sugar
- ¾ Cup of packed brown sugar
- 2 Eggs
- 1 Tsp. vanilla
- 1 1/3 Cups of all-purpose flour
- 1/8 Tsp. salt
- 1/8 Tsp. ground cinnamon
- Unsweetened cocoa powder and powdered sugar

**Cooking Instructions:**

1. Preheat oven to 350°F. Lightly grease a deep baking pan and keep aside. Combine chocolate, butter, and the water in a medium saucepan.

2. Cook and stir over low heat. Flip to a large bowl. Put granulated sugar and brown sugar in chocolate mixture and whisk with an electric mixer on low to medium speed.

3. Put eggs and vanilla and whisk on medium speed for 2 minutes. Put flour, salt, and cinnamon. Whisk on low speed. Sprinkle batter in prepared pan.

4. Bake for 30 minutes. Allow to cool in pan on a wire rack. Chop into bars. Drizzle with cocoa powder and powdered sugar.

5. Serve and enjoy!!!

# Cookie S'mores

Preparation Time: 10 minutes

Total Time: 10 minutes

Serves: 4

**Ingredients:**

- 16 Large marshmallows
- 8 Chocolate bars broken into quarters
- 16 Freshly baked chocolate chip cookies

**Cooking Instructions:**

1. Burn a fire and let the coals begin to turn ash. Put a marshmallow on a stick and roast over the glowing coals, stirring often.

2. When done, put on a cookie a quarter of the chocolate bar, top with the marshmallow and sandwich between another chocolate chip cookie and munch

3. Serve and enjoy!!!

## Stuffed Pizza Rolls

Preparation Time: 10 minutes

Cook Time: 25 minutes

Total Time: 35 minutes

Serves: 4

**Ingredients:**

- 1 Cup of grated mozzarella cheese
- ½ Cup of chopped broccoli
- Olive oil
- 2 Disks white wheat pizza dough
- 2/4 Cup of veggie-heavy pizza sauce

**Cooking Instructions:**

1. Preheat the oven to 400°F and oil the muffin cups. Roll out the pizza dough to ¼ inch thick.

2. Spread the marinara sauce in a thin layer across the surface of the dough. Sprinkle with the cheese and broccoli.

3. Roll up the dough to form a log and pinch the end together. Cut the log into pieces.

4. Put the pizza rolls in the muffin cups and pat down. Bake for 25 minutes.

5. Serve and enjoy!!!

www.ingramcontent.com/pod-product-compliance
Lightning Source LLC
Chambersburg PA
CBHW051806100526
44592CB00016B/2588